PERSONAL LEGACIES
Surviving the Great Depression

Books by Robin A. Edgar

In My Mother's Kitchen: An Introduction to the Healing Power of Reminiscence

Celebrating 20 Years and Growing

Object Stories: Written Accounts and Photography about Personal Heroes

Personal Legacies
Surviving the Great Depression

Charlotte / Mecklenburg
1929–1939

Robin A. Edgar

Photography by Jennifer Crickenberger

Illustrations by Jessi Godoy

Tree House Enterprises

©Copyright 2006 by Robin A. Edgar.
All rights reserved. No part of this book may be reproduced in any form or by any electronic or mechanical means, including information storage and retrieval systems, without permission in writing from the author.

Published by Tree House Enterprises
www.treehouseonline.net

Special thanks to *The Charlotte Observer* and The Charlotte Museum of History for permission to use photos from their archives.

ISBN: 978-0-9723770-8-9

Photography by Jennifer Crickenberger
Illustrations by Jessi Godoy
Cover concept by Kris Carmichael
Cover design by John Drake
Interior book design by Paragon Studios

Library of Congress Control Number: 2006931467

Printed and bound in the United States of America by CPCC Press
First Edition

 This project was made possible, in part, through the support of the North Carolina Arts Council, a state agency, the Blumenthal Endowment, and the arts councils in Cabarrus, Cleveland, Gaston, Iredell, Lincoln, Mecklenburg, Rowan, Rutherford, and York (SC) Counties.

Dedication

To my dear friend, Sam Gensler,
whose story of surviving the Great Depression and
how it shaped his life inspired me to write this book.

Hoskins neighborhood, West Charlotte circa 1936

Photo courtesy Earl Cox

Contents

Foreword	ix
Author's Note	x
Introduction	xi

1 Standing Together — 1
Evelyn Henderson Allen	3
Jesse Atkins	7
Sarah Brownlee Bryant	11
Price F. Davis	15
Ann Mauldin Elliot	19
Katie Stewart Grier	23
Bessie "Bett" Anderson Kofinas	27
Mary Anna McBride Turner	31

2 Working Through — 35
Jerome "Jerry" Levin	37
J. (James) Henry McGill	41
Martha Pegram Mitchell	45
Jean Surratt	49
R.D. Wike	53

3 Having Faith — 57
Dewitt Reid	59
Melvin J. "Skinny" Harris	63
Steve M. Karres	67
Virginia Hill Moore	71

4 Making Do — 75
Fred Orr Brown	77
Willie Stewart Coleman	81
Aubrey Federal	85
Cara Holbrook	89
Elizabeth Goodman Klein	93
Mary Worth Bonum McKain	97

Melba Ridenhour Moore	101
R. (Robert) Powell Majors	105

Facts, Figures & Photos
Charlotte / Mecklenburg
During The Great Depression 109

More Keys to Surviving the
Great Depression & Advice for
Future Generations 117

Afterword	127
Acknowledgments	128
The Author	129
The Photographer and the Illustrator	130
The Exhibit	131

Foreword

The Great Depression in Charlotte / Mecklenburg
1929–1939

There is a reason it was called the Great Depression. We have had many crashes, panics, and recessions, but never in recent memory was one so devastating and widespread as that which began in 1929. Not until ten years later, with the start of World War II, when thousands of draftees were taken out of the labor market and military production created jobs, did recovery begin from this terrible depression.

Statistics alone do not tell the story. It was a time when the banks themselves went bankrupt, when all one's savings were suddenly lost. There were no loans available, no social security nor other support programs to ease the misery. President Herbert Hoover stubbornly refused to feed destitute families, believing it would destroy their individual initiative and move the country toward socialism. Lacking tax revenues, cities and counties laid off firemen, policemen, sanitation workers, and teachers. Neither businessmen nor farmers could sell their products; factories closed and farms were mortgaged. Capitalism had failed!

Oral history can bring home to us the true reality of the Depression and its effect on families and individuals. Robin Edgar's book, concentrating on a cross-section of those living in the Charlotte-Mecklenburg area, should be especially relevant to Carolinians.

These stories, interesting in themselves, provide important lessons for our own times. They show how people, reduced largely to a system of barter and subsistence agriculture, found the means to survive. More importantly, the narratives reveal underlying values that gave this remarkable generation the ability to keep struggling. Those values carried through the Depression, and also through another ordeal—the outbreak of World War II.

Today, we live in a global economy of rapid technological change. Our country, deep in governmental and consumer debt, is once more economically fragile. Can we again respond successfully to dangers as overwhelming as the Great Depression? Let us read these narratives and take heart from them.

Norris W. Preyer
Dana Professor of History, Emeritus
Queens University of Charlotte

Author's Note

As a creative non-fiction writer, I use the principles of reminiscence to "find" stories. Utilizing an interactive sense-memory process to recall significant people and events in my writing workshops, I was inspired to write *In My Mother's Kitchen: An Introduction to the Healing Power of Reminiscence*. Since that time, I have been on a personal quest to get others to tell their stories, for their own sense of self-worth and for future generations to draw upon the wisdom and guidance inherent in those personal legacies.

Traveling around the country, teaching reminiscence workshops, I heard stories filled with wisdom and life lessons from individuals of all ages. It occurred to me, however, that the personal legacies of the older generation and how they made it through the hard times of the 1930s would be lost if we did not record them.

I approached Pam Meister, president and CEO of The Charlotte Museum of History, about creating an exhibit to record and display accounts of how people survived the Great Depression in Charlotte, North Carolina. Museum COO, Kris Carmichael and I developed a plan for a small hallway exhibit. The more we worked on it, the more excited we became.

Visiting nursing homes, breakfast groups, class reunions, and libraries around the greater Charlotte area, I used sense memory techniques from my book to help participants recall significant people, places, and events from the 1930s. More often than not, I interviewed the participants in groups, so that they could interact with one another and add their own ingredients to a communal "story stew."

Interviewing about ninety people, I tried to find representatives from various walks of life. Kris and I selected stories from twenty-five individuals for the exhibit. Rather than simply transcribing their interviews word for word, we decided that I should edit their comments into a story that included their family backgrounds as well as what they did after the Depression. In addition, I highlighted their life lessons for survival as well as their advice for future generations.

Through a Regional Artist Project Grant from the Charlotte Arts & Science Council, I was able to bring on photographer Jennifer Crickenberger to join me in these interview sessions to take individual portraits and to scan old family photos. Using images of the individuals, as well as objects, people, and places from their stories, she assembled photographic montages for inclusion in the exhibition. Incorporating repetition and visual distortion, Jen captured the essence of recollection.

What started as a minimal hallway exhibit eventually escalated into a full-scale exhibition with artifacts, interactive stations and more. The heart of it, the twenty-five stories and corresponding montages, appears in this volume. Although we could not include the stories of everyone that I interviewed, I included many of their comments in the section "More Keys to Surviving the Great Depression."

Introduction

This book explores ordinary histories during extraordinary times.

Since the beginning of time, storytelling has been used to explain our existence, preserve cultural history, and honor our ancestors. The repetition of these stories engenders a powerful connection to who we are and why we are here. They also cross barriers of race, gender, age and social strata.

History is not so much facts as it is documentation of points of view. Dr. James L. McGaugh explains in his book, *Memory and Emotion: The Making of Lasting Memories* (Columbia University Press), that the stress of an emotional event opens the passageways in the brain to consolidate long term memory. Are these long term memories completely accurate? Dr. McGaugh says not always. Certainly, they can shape your life as well as your world view.

Personal Legacies: Surviving the Great Depression utilizes sights, sounds, and smells to add living color to the black and white facts about the Depression Era. Unlike a straight oral history that simply records a verbatim account about how life was at the time, it also focuses on how individuals from various walks of life survived, and how that survival shaped their lives.

In addition to preserving and documenting the cultural history of the greater Charlotte area, these stories reflect life lessons and advice for future generations. Sharing these personal stories also acknowledges and celebrates the value and wisdom of our elders.

The book is organized into four chapters that represent the recurring keys to survival found in each of the stories. Although many of the stories have more than one message, they collectively state that the keys to survival involved: standing together as a community; working through the hard times; having faith in the Lord; and making do with what you have.

"Standing Together" reflects on how extended families and friends looked out for one another in the community. They forgave debts, watched each other's children, shared food and clothing, and took people into their homes.

"Working Through" illustrates how, with a die hard work ethic and a little ingenuity, people of all ages pitched in to keep a roof over their heads and food on the table. Shopkeepers worked long hours, farm families banded together to reap and mill their crops, and young boys sold newspapers and helped peddle wares.

"Having Faith" reveals how an inherent faith in God helped make mountains into molehills. Community church members looked after the needy, tent revivals inspired people to cast their cares on Him, and families that prayed together, stayed together.

"Making Do" demonstrates what people did to get by — from picking creasy greens and using every part of the pig, to making Hoover Buggies from defunct cars. Even on the tightest of budgets, families found ways to prepare meals, entertain themselves, and even manage to send their children to college.

Everyone has a story to tell. Hopefully, this book will inspire others to tell theirs!

Standing Together

EVELYN HENDERSON ALLEN

Born September 18, 1919

We were real lucky we had land and a large family that could help each other to survive during that time.

Evelyn Henderson Allen's paternal grandfather, Dallas A. Henderson, was born in Union County and moved to Mint Hill to open D.A. Henderson, a general store on Highway 218 off of Highway 51. He ran the store with the help of his two sons, Donald and John Dowd, Evelyn's father. Evelyn's mother, Lillian Morris, grew up on a farm in Mint Hill where Farmwood is today. She met John Dowd Henderson at the Bain Academy, the first school in the area, and they married after they graduated in 1910. They lived in a two-story house remodeled from a Woodsmen of the World Hall that was next door to John Dowd's parents, across the street from the general store.

In addition to selling food, clothing, shoes, farm equipment, and gasoline, John Dowd also ran a cotton gin in the back. During the Depression, it became harder and harder to keep the store open. People had no money so they bought on credit or would bring eggs in trade for sugar, flour, and mainstays.

> In 1933, my grandmother inherited land from her family below Mint Hill off of Brief Road. She divided the property among her children and Daddy decided to move us to the Beaver farm to raise hogs, cows, chickens, and cotton. We rented our house out to a math teacher at Bain's School and his wife.
>
> Uncle Donald went to work in Charlotte, so they tried to keep the store open with just Grandpa running it. That summer, I was just thirteen, but I worked in the store alone because we did not have much business and my grandfather was sick.
>
> We were real lucky we had land and a large family that could help each other to survive during that time. We all had chores to do. My sister and I helped with the housework and in the garden, and my brothers fed the horse and milked the cows. We made beds, washed dishes, and fed the chickens and the hogs. My mother used a churn, that was shaped like a cradle, to make butter. My brother would drive her to Charlotte to sell butter, eggs, and milk because people liked to get those things from the country.
>
> We did not do without food. We did not have a lot of clothes, but we had enough. My mother was able to make our clothes and my father bought our shoes at Belk's and Efird's when he went to Charlotte. Back then, you did not have but two pair of shoes, one for Sunday and one for everyday. We would save our clothes, wear something to school and take it off to do chores or go out to play.
>
> My father and his brother inherited the store when my grandfather died in 1933. They decided to close it. We knew everybody in Mint Hill and wanted to help them as much as we could. My father helped a lot of families and wrote off their bills when he closed the store. A year later, an uncle that lived in Morganton made an apartment over the store and lived there with his wife and family. They ran the store for several years until I graduated high school in 1936.

I got a job out of high school at Southern Bell in Charlotte. To get a job, you had to know someone and my doctor's brother was a top man in the company. I made forty dollars a month. At first, I stayed with an aunt and uncle in Charlotte and paid them five dollars a week room and board.

Evelyn was eventually able to get a ride from someone driving to Charlotte from Mint Hill and moved back home. In 1940, as the economy was picking up, she married her former classmate, Donald Dulin Allen. They had two children: Donnalea and Donald Denny. She says working hard taught her that she could take care of herself.

Her advice: "Do like my family did—work and help other people."

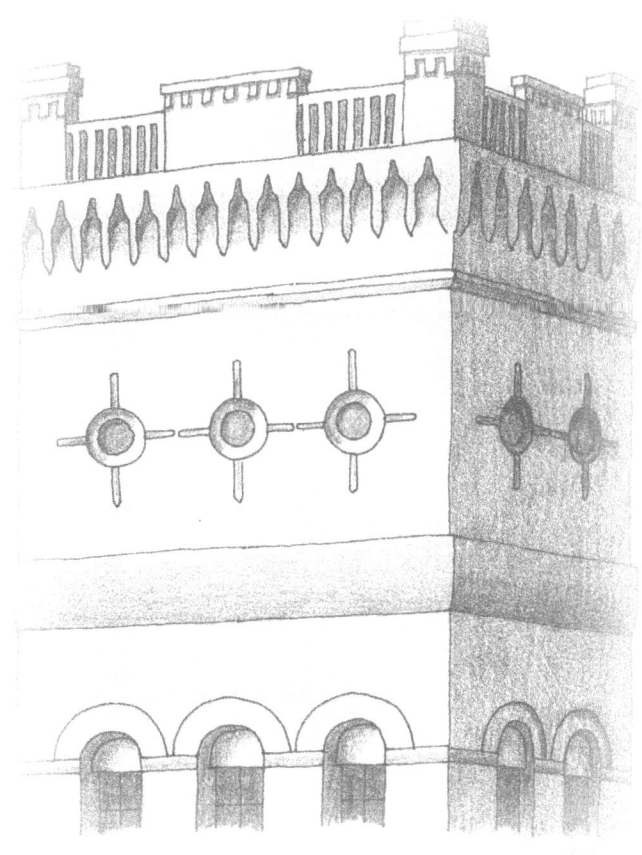

JESSE ATKINS

Born December 6, 1928

We survived because the mill village was a community of love.

Born in Pineville, Jesse Atkins was only three months old when his father left. His mother took a job as a spinner at the Highland Park Mill and they moved to Charlotte. Jesse's grandmother watched him while his mother worked from six in the morning until six at night for about seven dollars a week. They lived in a mill house on North Myers Street that had four rooms: a kitchen; a dining room, where the family spent most of their time during the day and used it as a bedroom at night; a front room that was also used as a bedroom; and a living room used for entertaining guests.

> My mother was Irish and her mother insisted that there was always a place for family to stay. Grandmother helped people in the neighborhood, too. They brought her cabbages for the community sauerkraut pot, a big wooden barrel with a board on the top and a rock to keep it down. She used to do wash for people in the wash pot in the backyard, boiling the clothes that she stirred with a big paddle. She also fed anybody who came by hungry. We had hobos come to the door from Bum Woods on the corner of Yadkin Avenue. Those hobos made some of the best stew you ever had in your life. Us kids were not supposed to go there, but we did.
>
> I went to school at North Charlotte Primary from first to third grade. It was a four-room school set off of North Davidson Street behind Spencer Memorial United Methodist Church, which is long gone. There were three classrooms and an auditorium. Most mill kids went to Tech High where the boys had wood shop, mechanical drawing, and auto mechanics. The girls had home economics.
>
> After school, we went to East 36th Street to the "park," which was where the Red Shield Boys Club was run by the Salvation Army. It was a big building that had a gym and a swimming pool.
>
> The mill villages were segregated, so we went to our own schools, but, when school was over, no one knew the difference. We were just kids. The families were mostly Scotch Irish and African American.
>
> It really wasn't a bad life. I had a wonderful time. It was all I knew. We did not know we were poor because everybody else was in the same boat. Nobody had any more than anyone else in the mill village. In the summer time, kids in the neighborhood knew what everyone was having for lunch and we could go to each other's houses.
>
> For entertainment we went to movies. Walking three miles to town along the railroad tracks, we would stop by Kress's on the way to pick up a five-cent bag of popcorn. I carried the *Charlotte News* for about three weeks for twenty-five cents a week to get enough to go to the movies. Then I delivered people's groceries from Barrett's grocery store across the street.

You could charge your groceries, have it taken out of your check, or pay for it. Mother paid for everything she got. She did not believe in charging anything if she could get out of it. She bought coal through the mill in the wintertime and the mill took it out of her salary.

She remarried, but my stepfather got fired for union participation so we moved a half block away from the mill village to 35th Street in 1939. We went from wooden floors to linoleum and thought we were really going up in the world. We also had a hot water heater that you fired up on Saturdays. The bathroom was on the back porch and we had a heater that you could fill with a bucket of coal in it at night and it was still warm in the morning. We raised a lot of food. We had a garden and chickens.

We survived because the mill village was a community of love. There was no getting by with anything. Teachers called your parents at work if you messed up. If you were at someone else's house and did something, they would correct you and then tell your parents. You learned to be self sufficient, as best you could, and to have moral values.

Jesse retired as a district fire chief after thirty years with the City of Charlotte. He says he wanted to be a fireman ever since he fell into the foundation of the Number Seven Fire Station on North Davidson during its construction in 1935. He married Johnsie Knight in 1948 and they had six children: Gwendolyn, Anne, Cindy, Joan, Jessie, and Timothy. A member of the Tech High Lunch Bunch, he also visits nursing homes, playing keyboard to entertain the seniors.

His advice: "The simplest thing in the world is to just love and respect people."

SARAH BROWNLEE BRYANT

Born May 8, 1922

I learned from watching my parents help people how much it means to give back.

Sarah Brownlee Bryant was born in St. Peter's Hospital. She lived in Dilworth until 1929, when her family moved to Grandin Road near the Wadsworth House. Her father worked for Lloyd Lumber at the time, but Mr. Lloyd committed suicide because of his losses from the Crash and his business closed. Fortunately, her father was able to get a job with Mr. Elrod's wholesale lumber business.

> I remember hearing about people jumping out of windows. Daddy lost money when the bank closed, but he had some investments in his father's farm in Georgia that helped us get by. He also managed his money very well. Although, he was very frugal, and we always thought he was stingy, I did not really feel that we were deprived. Somehow, he was able to keep the pain of the Depression from us. I did, however, lose the money that I deposited in the school bank program that was collected and deposited every week in the Independence Trust Company. (In the late 1930s, the bank refunded the money to the children.)
>
> Daddy traveled a lot, so weekends were special when he came home. On Saturdays we would go exploring in the woods and sometimes have a picnic in the country. On Sunday afternoons, we would go for drives around Charlotte, from little township to township.
>
> My mother stayed home with me, my sister Fran, and my brothers, Richard and Harry. She made our clothes and canned fruits and vegetables and saved up for a rainy day. I thought that was what everybody did.
>
> My Uncle Boyd lived with us, too. He had a radio that had earphones and we would sit in the living room and listen to *Amos 'n Andy* and the news that came on right around dinner time. In the summer, we would have tree-sitting marathons, an idea we got from hearing about dance marathons on the radio. We also had tea parties and played games with the neighbor children until our bedtime.
>
> In the winter, it would be cold, and only my parents' bedroom had a fireplace, so we used the stove in the living room to warm the blankets for our beds. We also put hot water bottles under the covers by our feet. My sister and I slept together in one bed. (I never slept in bed alone until I got to college.) We used to fight over the cover and pull on it and scream until my father would come in and trace an imaginary line with his finger down the middle to get us to stop—or else!
>
> We still had wonderful Christmases with a special meal served on the pretty china. Daddy's friend had a dairy farm and we would go out there to cut down a tree that we hung with lights and decorations made with strung cranberries and colored paper snowflakes. After church, we would entertain ourselves. My father loved to have my mother play Christmas carols and he would sing along with his deep voice.

For presents, we usually got dolls and fruit in our stockings. Once, my father made us a little table and chairs for our tea parties. My parents were always generous and thoughtful of people in need. We always took toys and clothes and food over to our maid's family for Christmas. There was a little boy who lived two blocks from us who did not get toys for Christmas because his father lost his job. I remember that my father took us shopping to buy some toys to take to him. He taught me that people who were poor were just like us.

I learned from watching my parents help people how much it means to give back. People came to the back door for food and mother never turned anyone away. She would always have some food to give them and clothes for the needy.

Sarah married Bob Bryant in 1942 and they had two sons: Jamie and Frank. Following in her parents' footsteps, she found ways to give back to her community, both as a pioneer for the first Planned Parenthood in North Carolina and as an active board member for over fifty years for Florence Crittenton Services. Sarah said the Depression years left their mark and that she always has to think before buying something because of her father's frugal ways. She said, however, "It was not all a loss, because we learned the value of family and friends."

Her advice: "Today, too much of our values are placed on material things, which can disappear, but families and friends last forever."

PRICE F. DAVIS

Born June 1, 1920

I used to hear my father tell my mother, "Let the kids eat, and if there is nothing left, we can drink some water."

Price Davis was born in Lincolnton, North Carolina. His father was a minister with the African Methodist Episcopal (AME) Zion Church. Both of his parents were teachers and they had to bid on a new school job every year. When Price's father became the principal of an elementary school, they moved from Taylorsville to Davidson. A few years later, he was promised a job in Charlotte and they moved to Providence Road by Queens Road. That job fell through, but he was able to get a position in Pineville six months later. He drove a horse and buggy there from Charlotte everyday to teach, but lost that job after the Crash and tried to get work on the construction crew for Providence Road.

>When Providence Road was first being built, mostly blacks were doing the work. Three or four months after the Crash, they put up a sign looking for workers that said, "Niggers and dogs need not apply." The Depression did not affect me as much as the racism did, which was much worse during that time. There was an Indian named Indian Bill that sat by Kress's and Belk's on Trade with a sign that said, "Whites first, Indians second, dogs third and Niggers last."
>
>When the Crash came, black people did not lose too much because they did not have that much to start with. The white people were hurt more, but blacks knew how to survive, how to put a little more water in the grits to make it stretch longer. I had an image of white men being mean and brutal, but I saw a different side of them during the Depression when I saw them cry because they had lost everything.
>
>All white people were not bad. They cried right along with black people. There was a white family on Providence Road, Mr. and Mrs. Love, that we called Mama and Papa because they would always come and bring whatever they had left over. Many black families had to work for white families in order to earn a living, even before the Crash.
>
>In 1933, Dad got a job teaching for Clinton Junior College in Rock Hill and my mother was able to quit working. We moved to the Cherry section on Torrence Street, which was the black neighborhood. Everyone stuck together. If you had beans and someone else did not have any food, you would wrap a few beans up in newspaper to send home with them. I used to hear my father tell my mother, "Let the kids eat, and if there is nothing left, we can drink some water."
>
>To help out at home, me and my brothers cut grass in Myers Park for ten cents an hour or a dollar a day with a mower we got from Sears for six dollars. One of my brothers built a car without a motor. When a reporter from the *Observer* saw us pushing it around, it reminded him of the Blackberry taxicab on *Amos 'n Andy*, and he took a picture of it for the paper. A white lady saw the article and she asked us to give her son a ride for his birthday. We pushed little

white kids around two or three blocks for two or three cents a ride.

You did whatever you could to have food—hunt rabbits, even when they were not in season, and throw rocks or use slingshots to get birds in the trees, even cardinals or blue jays. You'd fish in the ponds and pick blueberries, blackberries, and plums in the summer. There was a minister who was a drayman and he cleaned out basements and stores. When potatoes got eyes, he would clean the bins out, cabbage and oranges and apples the same. He would bring it to our house and dump it in the backyard. My daddy would go to the neighbors to tell them to come and get some food.

The Davis family still owns that house on Torrence Street. Price was a truck driver most of his life, so he never married. He says, when he was growing up, the church was the backbone of the neighborhood and there was only one family without both parents. Today, he says he sees mothers with ten children and no father and wonders what has happened to the African American family.

His advice: "If you come from a loving family, you can survive."

ANN MAULDIN ELLIOT

Born September 30, 1920

We were not rich in money, but we were rich in family.

When Ann Mauldin Elliot was born, her family lived on College Street in the College Apartments across from where McColl Center for Visual Art is today. (College Street got its name from the women's college, the forerunner of Queens University that was located there.) In 1921, her family moved to China, where her father took over a subsidiary for the textile company, Saco Lowell. Returning to the states in 1923, they were living in Boston when the Crash hit. Her family moved to New York and then back to Charlotte in 1933.

> As a child, I was far more aware of the suffering in the North during the Depression. A good friend of the family, a bank president in the Boston area, committed suicide. When I saw men shuffling along looking so down, I felt like my heart would burst wide open to see those people who had to put out their hands.
>
> Charlotte was more agrarian than up north so it was different to see farmers coming by in trucks with live chickens and vegetables and fruit. I was not used to that. A woman named Dora was our maid and she would pluck the chickens.
>
> There were sad things here, too. A very close friend from a prominent family lost his business and he never recovered mentally or physically. People would come to the back door for food. They drew a "Kind Lady" sign at our home with a silhouette of a cat to tell others who came to our back door that they would get food there.
>
> Fortunately, Daddy worked for a large textile machinery company and was never out of work. He came back south as southern sales manager, but there were upheavals, probably due to the Depression, and the reorganization changed the definition of his job somewhat. I was aware of the politics within the company and that probably turned me off to big companies.
>
> We were not rich in money, but we were rich in family. I was one of five children and my family was very close. My mother's sister lived with us for a year and we had to tighten our belts. I remember when Sloppy Joe sweaters, which came down to the knees, were in style and I asked my mother for one. I was so disappointed when she said, "Ann, you already have a sweater." We used to love mousse, but we cut down on luxuries, like cream, during the Depression. For a while, we had a Hudson and a Terraplane, but had to go to one car. That was hard on my mother with four different schools to drive her children to.
>
> Charlotte was a little town. We never locked the door or were afraid. When I missed my ride to Central High, I could walk to school across McDowell Street, which was a black community called "Blue Heaven" with no fear.
>
> We made our own entertainment. In our early teens, we had "prom" parties where we wore evening dresses and made artificial conversation to learn social graces. You had a card with ten-minute periods called "proms," but you did not

dance. The boys would sign up for a prom and we walked around the block and talked for ten minutes. I remember one time, I walked around the block with a boy named Jasper and we did not open our mouths one time.

Later, in high school, we danced a lot. The Big Band era was starting and the boys formed dance clubs. We had one or two dances a month, mostly at Myers Park Country Club before it was a fancy place.

In 1934, the North Carolina state schools went down to eight months a year with eleven grades to save money. When I was in the ninth grade, one of the churches campaigned for another month of school and to add back the twelfth grade. Some young church people organized a parade that started at St. Peter's Episcopal and went to Elizabeth. We had fun and carried banners and cheered. As a result, the city passed a bond in 1935 to give more money to city schools. I believe Charlotte and Asheville were the only cities in the state open for nine months and had twelve grades at one point.

Ann says her family was like a rolling stone, renting homes on Queens Road West, East Boulevard and then Dilworth Road East before her father finally bought a house on Wellesley in the 1940s. She married her high school sweetheart, "Pinky," in 1943 and they had four children: Jo Ann, Caroline, John Drew, Jr., and Robert. Still close to her siblings today, she says she continues to live by the thought that her richness is in the family.

Her advice: "The real values in life are the ones that stick with you. With family, not material things, you can do what life hands you."

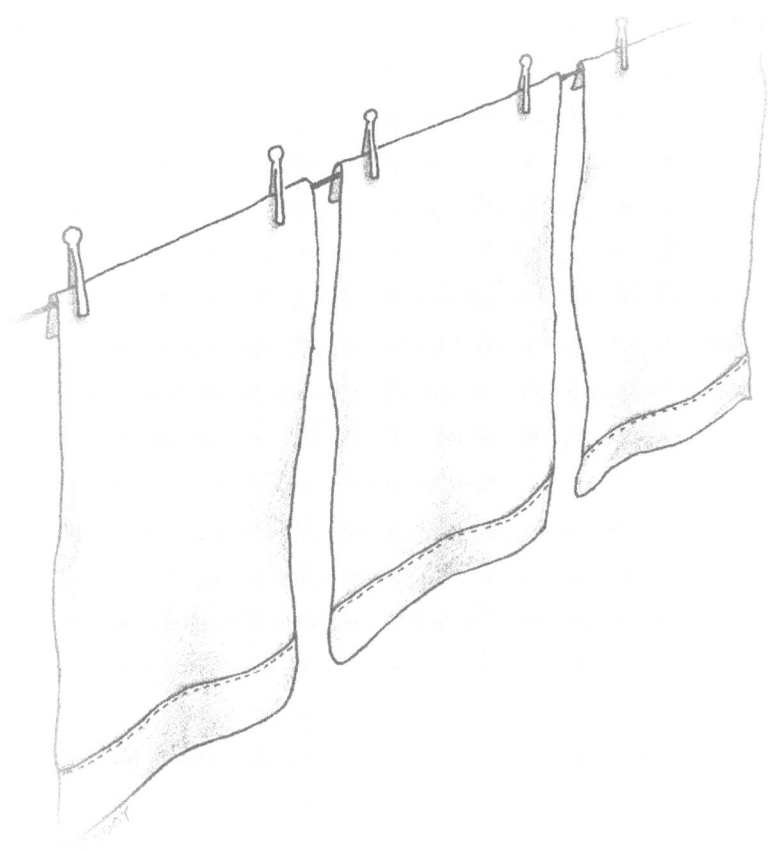

KATIE STEWART GRIER

Born June 1, 1925

We survived because everyone shared and looked out for each other.

Katie Stewart Grier was the oldest in a family of four boys and four girls. Her parents were sharecroppers on Tom Neely's farm, about twelve miles out of town in Steele Creek. They lived in a wood frame house with a porch. It had two rooms downstairs—the kitchen and her parents' bedroom—and several bedrooms sectioned off upstairs. They had their own garden where they grew beans, beets, okra, tomatoes, corn, and potatoes.

> I didn't know I was poor because we lived on a farm and we always had food. My dad was a smart old man. He raised most of the food for the family and saved money so he did not owe much to the farmer. We had cows for milk and a churn for making butter. We also had chickens and two hogs to raise pigs to sell. All we had to buy in the store was salt, sugar, and soda for baking. One year, the boll weevils ate the cotton that we had planted, so we did not get any money and we ate peas because that was all we had.
>
> Daddy would get us up at 5:00 A.M. and we would get our clothes on and start out. We had two cows, and Daddy milked one and I milked the other. Then we would have grits or mush for breakfast and carry our lunch of sausage and biscuits or baked potato to school. We walked about a mile and a half to get there. I remember going to school and coming home to work on the farm. We used kerosene lamps to do our homework.
>
> I was the oldest child and they treated me like I was grown with the responsibilities I had. My mother and father worked, so I started cooking when I was eight years old. I had to have dinner on the table for my parents and five kids. One of my chores was working the garden. I planted the seeds and weeded and kept the ground soft. We had to keep those weeds out of the garden. I hated that, but my daddy had to have it clean. I still weed my garden today, like my dad taught me to, but I don't hate it as bad now.
>
> I also helped wash clothes with the washboard. You had to get water from the well and then you heated the water in the wash pot on a stack of bricks with wood around it for the fire. On a bench that Daddy built, there were two washtubs, one for me and one for Mama, to wash and two tubs, with cold water, to rinse. After you rinsed them, you hung them on the line to dry. My mother made us hang every piece just right and even on the line. (When I got married I just threw the clothes on the line, but then I went back and did it the way Mama taught me.)
>
> We survived because everyone shared and looked out for each other. Back then, if someone had something and someone didn't, you shared it with them. When my dad killed a hog, he would send some meat to the other tenant farmers who were our neighbors. We used to help the older people by bringing them their wood, their water, and their mail. I got hand-me-downs from the daughter of a

lady named Annie Choat that my mother worked for as a domestic. Then, when I outgrew something, we would pass it on to a neighbor that had a child younger than me. My mother taught us not to waste and to make things last longer. I do that today.

Katie decided she was not going to live on a farm, so she married a city man and says she almost starved to death. She became a licensed practical nurse and raised five children: Howard, Bernell, Charles, Harold, and Jessica. She belongs to the Young at Heart group at the Wilmore Community Center and loves to make cakes, pies, and "stickies" for her family. She says she is concerned that people today do not share and are not as caring as they used to be.

Her advice: "Don't try to outdo each other. Share what you have."

BESSIE "BETT" ANDERSON KOFINAS

Born September 26, 1922

We were able to survive because of our family, relatives, and friends.

Bett Anderson Kofinas and her family moved from Philadelphia, Pennsylvania to Charlotte after her father's restaurant closed in 1931. A year later, her father died, leaving her mother with six children. With the help of relatives and a women's church organization called *Philoptochos* (Friends of the Poor), they were able to stay in their house at 1034 South Boulevard, across the street from the Pritchard Memorial Baptist Church. Only eight blocks from the Greek church, their home soon became the "Grand Central Station" of the Greek community.

> We were such a close-knit family and we always had company. Our house was a place where everybody wanted to come. Women also stopped over to have coffee before attending meetings at church. Most of the children attended Alexander Graham Elementary, a few blocks away. Since they had an hour before Greek school started, they all congregated at our house.
>
> Greek immigrants wanted their children to have a better education than they had, so they insisted that the younger generation attend school. They also sent them to the Greek school to preserve their culture and language. We had a rich culture and were fortunate to have leaders who knew something about music. We sang in the choir and put on plays in the Greek school. Our family had a record player so we taught the boys in the community to dance.
>
> Mother crocheted and baked things to sell, and people would bring her bolts of material and she used to sew all of our clothes. I remember she made sailor dresses when we were young. We were not fashion conscious. We just wore what she made. We went to school with some of the richest kids and did not feel any different. We had self-esteem because our parents instilled in us that we were special. We were Greek and proud of it.
>
> Family was what kept us together. On the holidays we always celebrated as a family. My mother baked and we sat together and prayed together as a family. That was most important. We all spoke Greek in our homes and had the mentality to carry out the Greek Orthodox holiday and heritage, but we did not live like they lived in the villages back in Greece. We lived like our neighbors did.
>
> When I look back now, I think the beauty of our community was that we did not think about where people came from. My mother associated with women from Turkey, but today there is a separation. Our parents feared they would lose what they had, so they kept the community bonds.
>
> We were able to survive because of our family, relatives, and friends. Part of our heritage was to support and take care of each other. The community was so loving and giving, and the church was the main focus of our family life. We had community picnics where all the families would gather and we would become one. The church always was first. If you did not participate, you lost your heritage.

In the 1940s, Bett served a term as president of the *Estia* Club, a young Greek girls organization that printed a publication to send to the local servicemen to keep them informed of community news. She married Kosmas Kofinas, who came from one of the first Greek families to move to Charlotte. Kosmas worked at the family fruit stand on West Trade Street and later opened the Kofinas Snack Bar near the Charlotte Hotel. Bett worked there as cashier and hostess while she raised their two boys, Steven and Gary.

Singing in the choir for twenty-five years, she continued to be involved with the church, serving as president on the Greek school board. She later became involved with *Philoptochos*, serving as president three times for the local chapter as well as for the diocese and the national board, and as president of the Daughters of Penelope. In the community, she was on the board of the YWCA, volunteered for the American Red Cross, and worked with the United Way.

Her advice: "Be active and belong to your church, whatever denomination. Hold on to your family ties; it means a lot."

MARY ANNA MCBRIDE TURNER

Born July 4, 1921

We were fortunate to have a large extended family that looked out for one another.

Mary Anna McBride Turner's maternal great-grandparents moved to Charlotte from Pennsylvania right after the Civil War. Her great-grandfather Liddell worked as a supervisor of a foundry, which later became the Liddell Company when he became a co-owner. Mary Anna was born in Charlotte and grew up in a four-bedroom house on Crescent Avenue (now Randolph Road). She attended Elizabeth Elementary School, Alexander Graham Middle School, and Central High School. Her father had an office job with the Highland Park Mill.

> My father, who came to Charlotte from Bambridge, Georgia, worked in the office of the Highland Park Manufacturing Company, a cotton mill in North Charlotte. (The building is now condominiums.) Among other things Daddy did, he handled the payroll, so he got along pretty well with the workers. He had to carry a gun for a while when he crossed the picket lines when the unions were trying to organize the mill. I know this because I saw the gun once when I opened the glove compartment. The mill had to close down for two years during the Depression, but the office staff was kept on. We were lucky.
>
> As children, we still had a lot of fun. My friend Kassie and I would go to the movies on Saturday. We each had a quarter to spend and the movie was a dime and the streetcar cost seven cents. We would always walk so we could spend the other fifteen cents at Nunally's drugstore to buy the best ice cream sodas. (We thought sherry flavor was so sophisticated.) Then we pooled our nickels to buy a bag of jellybeans to take to the movie.
>
> At Christmas, everybody got a gift for someone else, but they were simple gifts, not like people give today. We did not have a whole lot of money to spare, but things were much, much cheaper. (It astounds me that, nowadays, a woman of my age can carry a bag of groceries worth fifty dollars!) Mother gave us each a dollar to do our Christmas shopping at the dime store. I usually spent a nickel for everybody and a dime for each of my parents. I remember the salt and pepper shakers that I bought for my grandparents—a dog for my grandfather and the cat for my grandmother—for a nickel apiece. Modernistic was kind of in so they were very contemporary.
>
> Daddy used to go out in the country to get a cedar tree. We made some of our ornaments out of construction paper, but we also had some that had been handed down by the family.
>
> There were Christmas lights on the Square and we loved to go uptown to have lunch at the S&W and look at all of the store windows of the department stores like Belk's, Ivey's, and Efird's (they had the first escalator). The stores were owned by local families and they would deliver your purchases to your

house because you usually went uptown on the streetcar.

Everybody talked about the Depression. My earliest memory was going to a parade to bury Old Man Depression. (Daddy loved parades.) After the parade, I was surprised because the Depression kept going on.

The saddest thing during the Depression was that a lot of people could not get jobs. We were fortunate to have a large extended family that looked out for one another. At Christmas time, we always gave a little something to the Empty Stocking Fund and to the Salvation Army person who stood on the corner with the bell and big kettle.

After graduating from Florida State College for Women (now Florida State University), Mary Anna did graduate studies in art history at the Institute of Fine Arts at New York University. Returning to Charlotte, she worked for ten years in the art department at the Charlotte Engraving Company before she married James Turner. They had one daughter, Mary Anna. Determined to play an active part in her community, she was a volunteer at the Mint Museum of Art for twenty years, and is now a volunteer at the Urban Ministry soup kitchen and at Discovery Place. Fascinated with the way Charlotte is growing, Mary Anna says she loves everything about it except the traffic.

Her advice: "Nowadays, everybody tries to go to school to learn how to make money. What people really need to learn is how to spend money wisely."

Working Through 2

JEROME "JERRY" LEVIN

Born October 25, 1924

We worked long hours and did not spend money if we did not have to.

Jerry Levin's maternal grandparents, David and Lena Lebowitz, moved to Gastonia before the turn of the century and opened a department store called Lebo's. Jerry's parents, Tina and Sidney Levin, had the first Jewish wedding in Gastonia in 1922. Moving to Charlotte, they lived opposite an old fire station on the side of the courthouse by Fourth and Caldwell Streets. His father bought two shoe stores under a hotel on East Trade and Tryon Streets, naming the moderately-priced store, Lebo's after his father-in-law's store. He named the one that carried high-end shoes, Herbert's. He eventually opened up three more stores, but closed all of them except Lebo's when the Depression hit because most people could not afford high-end shoes.

> It was a struggle just to keep that one going and to make ends meet. There was no free ride for anybody. We worked long hours and did not spend money if we did not have to. My mother brought my father lunch every day because he would not spend a quarter to buy it. She would help watch the store while he ate his lunch during the week and she also worked there on the weekends.
>
> We moved to a house on Colonial Avenue right before the Depression hit. Money was tight and we didn't have a lot of assets, but we felt we did because we had each other. As kids, we took buckets of coke on our bikes and sold them to the workers for a nickel apiece. My mother made me save it, and when I wanted to buy something, I had to use some of my money, too.
>
> I walked with my sister to Elizabeth School, about eight blocks away. One woman gave me a quarter a week, which was a lot of money at that time, to walk her little boy, too. I used the money to go to the State Theatre, where they had western serials every week and you got popcorn, the movie, and a drink for a quarter. I could also go to football games on Fridays at Central High School for a quarter.
>
> Everybody was struggling to pay the bills and put food on the table, but no one knew they were poor. People had a lot of pride and did not go on relief. It was a stigma to do that.
>
> My dad had a heart of gold. He always helped the downtrodden. One family, customers before the Depression, came in and did not have money to buy shoes, much less heat the house. Dad gave them money for kerosene for the heater and gave the kids shoes. They came back years later and paid him back and the family still shops with us. There were many stories like that. I have people tell me today that their parents said Lebo's is the only place to buy shoes because they are treated with respect and courtesy, regardless of wealth, color, or creed.
>
> In the 1930s, a group of us walked from Alexander Graham Junior High School to the temple on Seventh Street three days a week to learn Hebrew and the

services for our bar mitzvah ceremonies. My bar mitzvah was held in 1937.

Temple Israel started out in Charlotte as a brotherhood in 1895. They did not have a rabbi until they hired Rabbi Greenberg in 1930. It was a very small Jewish community with maybe 125 members and they struggled to pay him $12,000 a year and he was lucky to get that. He was everything: cantor, teacher, speaker, and rabbi.

A majority of the Jewish people were Orthodox in belief, but not in practice, because they were in the retail business. Saturday (the Jewish sabbath) was a big retail day when mill workers and farmers would come in town to shop. Besides Saturdays, we were open from eight in the morning to six at night during the week and until nine at night on Fridays.

I walked from Central High to town to work at Lebo's after school and I also worked on the weekends. That is how I learned the business and, by sixteen, I was a salesman. I also made seven dollars a week delivering about one hundred weekly magazines, such as *LIFE* and the *Saturday Evening Post* to the doctors, lawyers, and barbers downtown. I learned to appreciate the work ethics you needed to survive and to build a family.

Jerry still runs Lebo's shoe store on Independence Boulevard today. He and his wife, Barbara, have four children: Bruce, Linda, Nancy, and Susan. In keeping with his father's example, Jerry is active in community affairs. He serves as co-chairman for Charlotte Federation of Jewish Charities, is an honorary life-president of Temple Israel, and participates on several other local and national boards.

His advice: "The best way to live is to get known and to get involved."

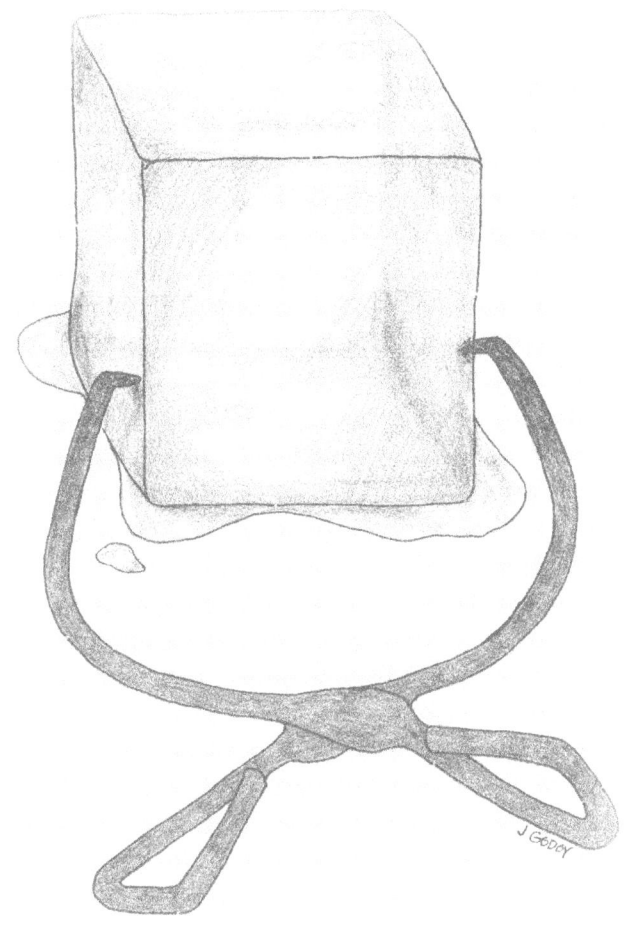

J. (JAMES) HENRY MCGILL

Born August 7, 1903

You didn't have any trouble getting someone to work for you because anyone applying for a job did not ask how much they would get; they just wanted the work.

J. Henry McGill was born in Bethany, South Carolina. He attended Erskine College in Due West, South Carolina and transferred to Massey School of Business in Richmond, Virginia where he received a degree in banking 1926. He worked for Farmer's Bank and Trust in Richmond before he moved back home to work for People's Bank and Trust in York. He worked there for less than a year before it closed in 1927. The Depression hit South Carolina before the rest of the country, so Henry moved up to Charlotte because his father had a friend who could get him a job with Commercial Bank. Earning $37.50 a week, he lived in a duplex on East Kingston Street.

In 1929, after he married his college sweetheart, Helen Moffatt, Henry decided to get out of the banking business. He heard that five of the ice delivery companies in town were concerned about the arrival of the electric refrigerator and had consolidated to form City Ice Delivery to avoid competition. In 1930, he became their delivery manager for $350 a month, about $50 more a week than he was making at the bank.

> I had about one hundred drivers working for me. They were fortunate that they were able to keep most of their jobs. You didn't have any trouble getting someone to work for you because anyone applying for a job did not ask how much they would get; they just wanted the work.
> One day, I was having lunch at home when the office called me and told me to come over because the drivers were on strike for more money. As I got in my car to drive down to meet with them, I didn't know what I was going to say. When I got there, they were sitting outside in the street with their trucks unloaded, waiting for me.
> I knew the ringleader. He was a splendid driver and it would have been hard to replace him. I told them that they had all received favors from me and the company before, but I could not give them any more money. Then I said that they had thirty minutes to either reload and to get on their trucks or they could go to the office and pick up their checks. I was bluffing because I did not have the money to pay them if they quit. I guess they were bluffing, too, because the ringleader was the first one to move and reload and the others followed.
> Back home, my family struggled to keep their small country store running. Competition from the big stores closed down my father-in law's wholesale grocery business during the Depression, just like the big-box stores are putting the small guys out of business today. When I read in the papers nowadays about the banks and other companies letting people go so they can cut down on expenses and make more money, I can't understand why they do not see it. It will be just like it was during the Depression, when the farmers had no money to pay their bills.

By the early 1950s, Henry went out on his own and bought Avant Fuel & Ice Company. His wife, Helen, eventually planted more than 500 rosebushes in that fuel yard, turning it into what is now known as the McGill Rose Garden. Helen passed away in 1985. A few years later, Mr. McGill got tired of staying home alone, so he joined the Fred Astaire Dance Studio, where he met his second wife, Joy. They live in the same house that he had built in 1936.

His advice: "You have to be able to see what is coming next and move on to the next thing."

MARTHA PEGRAM MITCHELL

Born November 1, 1917

If you were going to eat, you had to work to make it available.

T he old Neel family farmhouse in Steele Creek where Martha Pegram Mitchell was born was built before the Civil War. The members of her family tree, the Stowes, the Crowells, the Pegrams, and the Coopers, moved to the Steele Creek area from Virginia in the early 1700s. Although her father was very smart, he could not get advanced schooling because, as one of seventeen children, he had to help out on the farm. After he died in 1926, Martha, the youngest of seven children, had to pitch in with everyone else to help.

> We were always poor but, during the Depression, it was much worse. Everyone had to kick in and do. From the earliest moment I can remember, everyone had a chore to do like feed chickens or set tomato plants. If you were going to eat, you had to work to make it available.
>
> Soon after my father's death, my mother became a companion to several elderly people in town who paid her to help them. My older sister and her husband ran the household and my older brothers ran the farm. We were able to make do. Mother sewed my clothes from hand-me-downs from her sister and aunt. We had fruit trees, so she canned a lot of fruits and vegetables. My job was to wash the jars. I made a vow that I would never put anything in a jar again.
>
> Some people had a little more than others, but nobody had very much. We were all in the same boat. A black family that lived across the road helped my brothers with the farm work and my mother with the wash. They each made a dollar a day. I had to bring them water when they hoed the cotton in the field and I loved to hear them sing.
>
> We weren't hurting for food, but we had no money. Kids were not paid for chores because everybody's participation was necessary to keep the ship afloat. I would save from one year to the next just to have a quarter so I could buy five ice cream cones for a nickel apiece at our annual church summer picnic.
>
> For Christmas we would get a book or a sweater or underwear. It was all very practical things. I don't ever remember buying a gift for my mother. We helped her make fruitcake and other goodies. We always chopped down one of the cedar trees that grew on the farm and decorated it with paper chains that one of my older sisters made with flour paste. Friends of my father used to hunt birds on the property in the fall so they would bring us a crate of oranges and apples, a stalk of bananas, raisins dried on the branch, and some hard candy and nuts for the holiday.
>
> From time to time, I would feel tired of not having money. We were well fed, but we just didn't have a lot of things. We had a wall phone like in Mayberry, and outdoor plumbing. I was envious of my friend Margaret Winchester's short camel coat and of other people's cars compared to our old Ford Model A. I remember

being disappointed that I could not go to the senior play when I graduated high school because it cost a quarter and Mother did not have one to spare. That particular year must have been pretty hard, but she did manage to make me a new dress for graduation, which became my Sunday dress all summer.

I borrowed money from my sister's husband, who owned a shoe store in Salisbury, to go to nursing school in the late '30s. My brother would send me a dollar every couple of weeks so I could buy a coke and a Mr. Goodbar for a nickel apiece from the drugstore down the street. That was my treat.

Martha married during World War II when she was serving as an army nurse. Her husband escaped a POW camp just as the war ended and they moved to Charlotte. When their two daughters Lee and Ruth, and their son, Gregory, were older, Martha went back to work as a nurse at Presbyterian Hospital until she retired as a night supervisor. She volunteered as a driver for sixteen years and now coordinates errand transportation for the Shepherd's Center.

Her advice: "Give your very best effort in whatever you do. If you worked for it and earned it, you could hold your head high."

JEAN SURRATT

Born October 1, 1921

I realized that, if I persevered, I could overcome the bumps that I could not change.

Jean Surratt was born at home on Jackson Avenue, across from Piedmont Junior High School near Central Avenue. Both of his parents came from farm families—his father from Davidson County, and his mother from a family of nine girls and six boys in Statesville. His father drove a truck in the Quartermaster Corps in France during World War I and drove for the Frederickson Trucking Company when he returned. His mother worked as a nurse before she had children.

> Dad started his own trucking line, but it went broke about three times. We never had a whole lot of money and what we had went to food, so we did not always have money to pay the rent. Most places, you could rent the first two months for free, so we moved about twenty-six times from the time I was born until I was a senior in high school in 1940.
>
> We had hard times, but I saw people who were worse off than us. The colored people did not have near as much as we had and we had practically nothing. Because we always lived in town, we would always see a lot of men looking for work. They would come to our house for food after riding the freight trains from town to town. Even though we did not have money for rent, we shared what food we had.
>
> We ate a lot of beans and soup and homemade biscuits. We took fried chicken and biscuits to school for lunch, and for dinner, we had meatloaf with fried fruit pies for dessert. The black people would bring produce into town on mule-drawn wagons and call out what they had. It was anything they could grow, usually okra, turnips and collard greens. We bought eggs from them, too. Our milk was delivered and set on the front porch. Other vendors came through on wagons and old trucks selling cans of coffee, pots and pans, and such.
>
> Mother came from a farm family, so she was self-sufficient. Farm kids worked all of the time. She was three years old when they turned a bucket upside down so she could stand on it to wash dishes. She washed clothes on a washboard in a tub with Octagon soap and would dry them in the yard in the nice weather and in the kitchen or on the back porch when it was cold. She got quite good at sewing because she had to.
>
> When I was fifteen years old, we moved to Villa Heights in the Plaza area, where I started delivering for the *Charlotte News* in the afternoon. My first route was on Harold Street and I made about three dollars a week, which I shared with the family to buy food. (Money went a long way then.) A few times, I was among the boys who won a three-day trip to Myrtle Beach for getting the most new customers.
>
> Later on, I got a route with the *Observer*, which was delivered in the

morning. They dropped the papers off on the corner of Parkwood and Pegram Streets at about 4:00 A.M. and a "late man" would come by to check that you had picked up your papers before a certain time. If you didn't, you were fined twenty-five cents. I would deliver my papers and go home and take a nap before school started at 8:00 A.M.

There were a lot of deadbeats that did not pay for their papers. I made eight dollars a week for the *Observer*. We would pay thirteen cents for a week's worth of papers and customers would pay twenty cents. If someone did not pay us, it came out of our profits. One time, when a paper kept disappearing from the same house every morning, I hid in the bushes and watched a man a few houses down send his little boy over to steal the paper.

Delivering those newspapers taught me to be responsible and to give people proper customer service. I realized that, if I persevered, I could overcome the bumps that I could not change. I learned how to be thrifty and to be careful with my money. Going to church was also important because I believed in God and He helped me.

Jean was so tired of moving that, by the time he was seventeen or eighteen years old, he had saved enough money to pay $275 down on a 1,000 square foot three-bedroom, one-bath house on Thomas Avenue. He rented it to pay the mortgage, but the renters only stayed for two months, so his family moved in and his father made the payments. In 1944, he married his first wife, Betty, and had two daughters, Sherry and Cathy.

His advice: "Save money; don't buy everything you want."

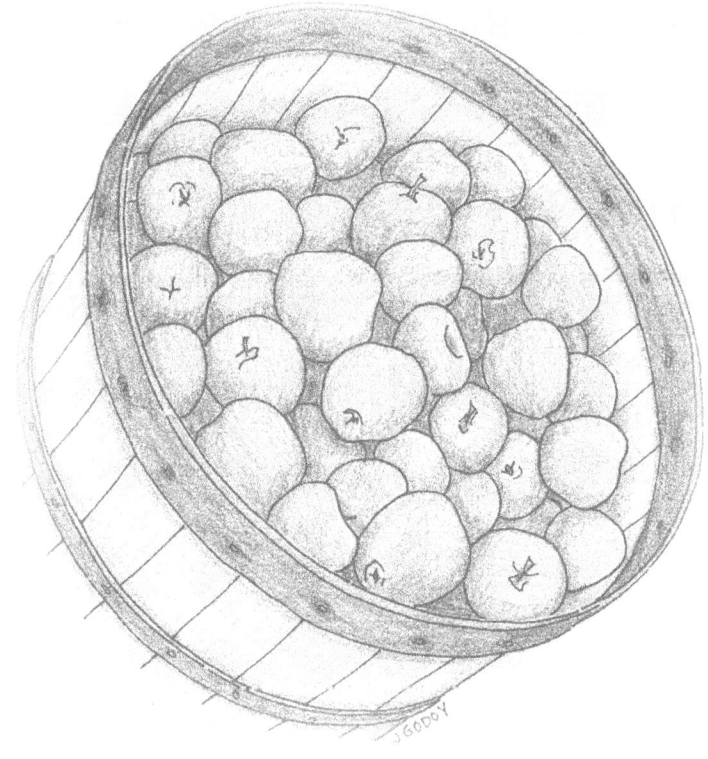

R.D. WIKE

Born December 20, 1926

You could sell anything, even an apple with rotten spots, because most of it was good.

R.D. Wike was born in Taylorsville, where his grandfather Ely Monroe Wike had one of the first Star King apple orchards in Alexander County. His father, Poley Crouch Wike, supported the family as a trucker, hauling apples from Taylorsville to Charlotte, where he sold them to the grocers and on the street. After the Depression hit and his father could not get as much money selling apples, the family moved to Charlotte, near Statesville Road. They continued to sell apples as well as other produce.

> The 1920s were good years until the Depression, when it was hard to make a living. We had to rent and we lived about a year in one place and moved into another. There were six boys at home during that time. My parents had nine children all together. I was next to the oldest and I liked to work. We had chickens and one or two cows to milk and I also had a job milking cows for our neighbor. He was a really good man and paid me when he could, but he simply did not always have the money.
>
> Five of the boys helped sell apples on North Tryon where the Sears & Roebuck store used to be. I sold many a half a peck there. Not too many people had fifty cents to buy a peck, so we sold an eight pound bucket for twenty-five cents to the poor people. At that time, you took a little less for an apple with a spot, but the person getting it was happy to get an apple for a little less money.
>
> You could sell anything, even an apple with rotten spots, because most of it was good. Selling apples taught me to be honest.
>
> My mother and father were both hard workers, but my mother, Mary Elizabeth, was a jewel. She took care of everything. She worked all the time. Growing up on a farm in Alexander County, she made a lot of pies, especially peach and apple. She really knew how to make pies, especially apple. We also ate applesauce and dried apples, which was a big thing at that time. (You sliced them real thin and put them on a screen to dry in the sun.) My mother would go out to the field and pick the cotton that we grew. We had a big garden and she would can anything she could get. One time, she had one hundred half-gallon jars of beans, squash, tomatoes, kraut, cucumbers, and whatever else she could get out of the garden.
>
> Back then, radio was a big thing. Not everybody had one, but my daddy got a used one for about six dollars. You could get a new one for eighteen dollars back then. I remember that I used to listen to *The Lone Ranger*. My daddy also bought me a used guitar and I taught myself how to pick it.

R.D. played guitar for a hobby most of his life. He married Mary Pelt in 1953 and had two children, Wayne and Bonnie. He owned a small trucking company until he retired in 1991. Although he always gave to his favorite church-related charities, he says living through the Depression gave him a big ambition to save what he could.

His advice: "The best thing to do with the money you make is to save what you can."

Having Faith

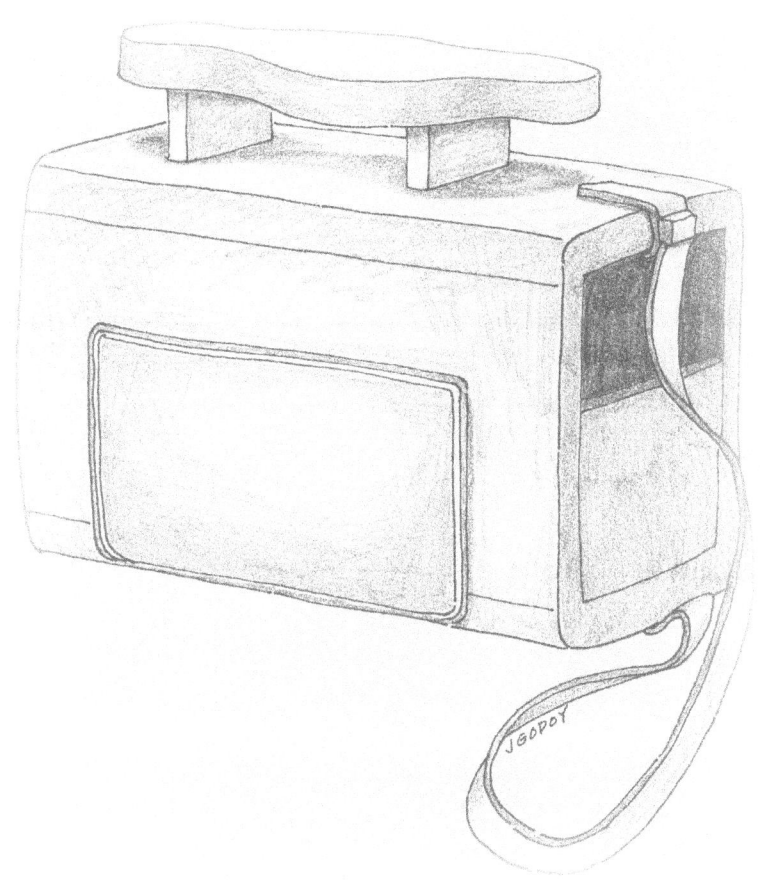

DEWITT REID

Born March 30, 1927

We survived because we had morals, discipline, individual family pride, and faith in the Lord.

Dewitt Reid was born, in Biddleville, an all-black community on Carmel Street on the west side of Charlotte. Near Johnson C. Smith University (formerly Biddle Memorial Institute, then Biddle University), it was just south of Washington Heights, which was the end of the trolley line that ran along Beatties Ford Road to the center of Charlotte on Mint Street. In 1932, his family moved to the Greenville section on the west side near the warehouse district.

> There were no paved roads in the black communities, except Mill Road in the Biddleville section. Black families lived in the wards that were built around the city so they could walk to work. Even though the buses only cost seven cents, they did not come through the black community. Gas was about sixteen cents a gallon and taxis only charged ten cents to go to town.
>
> Very few blacks were employed during the Depression. My dad worked for an invalid, Mr. Flynn, who was a person of means that lived in the city on Fifth Street. Mom worked as a domestic for a Jewish family on Central Avenue, named the Pliners. They owned a furniture store on the corner of College and Trade. My grandmother worked for Ben Douglas, who was the mayor at the time.
>
> My family lived in a shotgun house and we shared an outhouse with four other families. You brought your own newspaper for toilet paper and sometimes you had to wait in line. We would go down to the creek to get the white clay that formed on the banks to whitewash the inside and under the outhouses to sanitize them.
>
> Nobody ever went hungry because we could pick "creasy greens" (similar to watercress) by the creek banks and "poke salad" (pokeweed) by the mine hill. Mama made fatback gravy out of salt pork and used fish heads to make stew. We walked to Merita Bakery on West Trade Street to get week-old bread and ate it, mold and all.
>
> When people were desperate for heat in the winter, they would walk along the railroad tracks looking for pieces of coal that fell off the cars. Boards that fell off an empty house were used for firewood. When the WPA came to clean up an area, people would take wood from their piles or rummage for wood in the garbage dump on the west side of town (now known as Double Oaks).
>
> I was the oldest, with one brother and one sister, and I worked before I was ten years old to help out my family. My first job was delivering handbills door to door from stores like Sears, JC Penney, and Belk's, and from food stores like Big Star, A&P, and Colonial. I made thirty-five cents an hour. On Saturday mornings, we would deliver in Gastonia and, after walking the entire length of Franklin Avenue, I would get lunch: a can of pork and beans, a can of potted meat, a honey

bun, and a bottle of soda similar to a Coke called a "three-center."

When I was ten years old, I started to shine shoes on the street until they required a dollar a year for a license. After that, I just left my shoeshine kit by the corner at the fire station and the firemen would use my stuff and leave me money. I built a wooden wagon with discarded wheels from the mills and went all over town looking for copper and aluminum to sell for five cents a pound at the Schwartz junkyard where the stadium is now. Sometimes, I went to a produce place, where the Eckerd's warehouse is now, and rode the trucks loaded with apples to sell in the affluent communities like Myers Park. I made five cents for every peck that sold for twenty-five cents.

The whole community took care of us. Because it was cohesive and small, there truly was no child left behind. We had a small country church and small stores. When times were tough, you could run up a grocery tab. People today could not survive with big-box stores putting small stores out of business. We survived because we had morals, discipline, individual family pride, and faith in the Lord.

Dewitt received several grants from the National Science Foundation and pursued a degree in education from Fayetteville State University in North Carolina and did further studies at Brooklyn College in New York. He married Lucille Brown and had a daughter, Yvonne. After teaching in the Charlotte school system for twenty years, he worked as an Equal Opportunity Officer for Duke Power. Now retired, he returned to the school system as a substitute teacher because he is concerned for the students. He estimates that fifty percent of the young people he teaches do not live with their parents. He says, "Without a strong sense of family or community, the students have no social skills or respect."

His advice: "Learn to respect those who are older and who have more wisdom and experience."

MELVIN J. "SKINNY" HARRIS

Born October 19, 1920

My family taught me to trust the Good Lord and I have done that all my life. Just put him first and you never have to worry.

Melvin J. "Skinny" Harris' grandfather Nathaniel J. Harris was a Methodist minister, so the family moved to a different location every few years. Skinny's father, Samuel, was born in England and came to the United States when he was three years old. When they lived in Detroit, his father met Nina Pearl Wright. They married in 1915 and Samuel took a job, sight unseen, in the undertaking business. The couple moved to Union, South Carolina.

In 1922, his partner left with the company bank account, so Samuel took a job in Charlotte with the Perry Mincey Furniture Company. The family moved to Jackson Avenue when Skinny and his brother Merle went to Elizabeth Elementary School. They were close enough to walk home for lunch, which saved the family money during the Depression years.

> Mother thought she came to the end of the world because there were no paved roads. She stayed home to raise the family and I always held women on a pedestal because that is the hardest job with no pay. Our grandparents still lived in Detroit and we did not see them in those days. Every so often, my grandmother would send us the funnies from the *Detroit News*. They were in color and we really enjoyed them.
>
> When I was ten years old, I sold magazines—the *Saturday Evening Post* and *Ladies Home Journal*,—in order to purchase a bicycle. That was the only way I had to raise the money. My family taught me to trust the good Lord and I have done that all my life. Just put Him first and you never have to worry. So, when my folks took my brother and me to a Hamm and Ramsey tent revival meeting, I was so touched by the Lord that I figured He needed the money more than I did. I gave Him all the money and I never did get a bicycle.
>
> I was always interested in music and was in the band, orchestra, and glee club in school. In 1938, the year I was supposed to graduate, I found out that Central High School was going to offer a class in theory and harmony the following year. One of my classmates, Bobby Trotter, and I decided not to receive our diplomas so we could to go back to Central High the next year. We took all the music classes we could because there was no money to go to college.
>
> In 1939, I got my first job at Ed Mellon's Men's Clothing Store. I wrapped packages behind the counter for six days a week and made thirty dollars a month. Nothing was taken out of the check. I was very thrifty. If I didn't have the money, I didn't buy it. My grandfather taught me a fantastic lesson. He had a saying: "It's awful hard to pay for a dead horse."

Today, Skinny says the only thing he owes is to the Good Lord and he owes everything to Him. He still plays music in a Dixieland band called Southern Fried Jazz and he has been playing clarinet and tenor banjo in a trio twice a week at the Cajun Queen restaurant on

East Seventh Street for seventeen years. He married Nancy Allen and had two daughters, Linda and Donna. Recently widowed after fifty-nine years, he married a dear friend, Helen May, whom he and his wife had known for fifty years. He says the Lord looks after him and, although he never got a bicycle, he now has a Grand Marquis.

His advice: "If you cannot afford cash to pay for it, don't purchase it."

STEVE M. KARRES

Born September 27, 1920

The members of the Greek community survived because there were no factions; we were united.

Steve M. Karres' parents came from Karyae, a Greek village near Sparta. His mother, Maria Petroulias, came to America as a young girl and lived with an older brother and his wife in Dabny, South Carolina. His father, Matthew Karres, journeyed to Durham, North Carolina when he was eleven years old to live with his older brother, Nick, who had a business across the street from Trinity College. Nick befriended Trinity's president, Dr. Few, who took Matthew under his wing and taught him how to read and write.

When Matthew graduated from high school, he worked for Nicholas Trakas, an older gentleman from Karyae who lived in Spartanburg, South Carolina. After starting his own wholesale grocery business in Asheville, Matthew moved to Charlotte in 1920 to form Southern Fruit Company, Inc. with two close friends from Karyae. Specializing in fresh fruits and vegetables, they serviced restaurants, grocery stores, hotels, cafeterias, and hospitals.

By 1924, there were fifty-seven Greek families in Charlotte. Most of them worked in the restaurant business.

> The people of our community were very proud of their heritage. They spoke Greek at home and sent their children to afternoon Greek school several days a week to learn to read and write in Greek. Until we had our own church building, we held our weddings and christenings in the old Chamber of Commerce on West Fourth Street. We held Easter services in St. Peter's Episcopal Church the years that our Easter did not fall on the same day as theirs.
>
> My father and his associates formed the Hellenic Orthodox Community to promote, preserve and maintain a Greek community church. In 1929, the community purchased the Westminster Presbyterian Church on South Boulevard for $32,000 and renamed it Holy Trinity Greek Orthodox. An Orthodox church in Baltimore, Maryland sold us their icons and other fixtures for $500.
>
> The members of the Greek community survived because there were no factions; we were united. Everybody had one objective, the church. Many of the Greek men had to work in their businesses on Sundays so, during the depths of the Depression, the teenagers walked up and down Trade, College, Graham, and Tryon Streets with a piggy bank to ask those parishioners for donations to help maintain the church.
>
> We tried never to take financial help from anyone but the Greek community. Those who were able contributed to the altar fund that the priest used to help the needy. The ladies in the community formed *Philoptochos*, "Friends of the Poor" in 1931. If there was a needy family, the community came together. One would say, "Send the electric bill to me." Another would say, "Send the water bill to me." Families were very proud, so when someone was in dire need, people would take groceries to their house at four or five o'clock in the morning, so no one

knew where it came from.

Everybody showed up at christenings and weddings. No one needed an invitation. People served pastries like *kourambiethes*, a sugar cookie, and fruit preserves made from cherries and pears. They also served demitasse coffee and drinks such as *ouzo* and *mastika*. During the Lenten season, they served fresh fruit like honeydew melons, cantaloupes, and grapes.

Charlotte was a delightful place to live and grow up. It was a small town and we had a very good school system. We all were involved with sports and music, so you met and knew everybody.

Steve received the Civitan Citizenship Award for his service as president of the Senior Class and the Student Body when he graduated Central High in 1939. He graduated from UNC at Chapel Hill, where he was a member of the Golden Fleece and the Holy Grail. Working for Southern Fruit Company as the secretary-treasurer until 1953, he worked for the Fruehauf Corporation until he retired as the vice president of fleet sales. Still active with the church, Steve divides his time between Charlotte and Blowing Rock with his wife, Mary, their sons, Matthew and Christopher, and his friends from Central High and Chapel Hill.

His advice: "The family is the greatest thing of all."

VIRGINIA HILL MOORE

Born February 4, 1915

My sister Louise used to pray, "Dear God, we thank you for what we have, but could you squeeze out a little bit more?"

Virginia Hill Moore was born about four miles south of Hamlet, North Carolina. Her father, Lattie Van Hill, was a preacher and a blacksmith. He died in the 1918 flu epidemic, leaving her mother, Rebecca, to provide for six children.

Virginia's husband, Horace Moore, was born on a rice farm in Georgetown, South Carolina, but went to work in the mills when farming got bad in the late 1920s. He eventually moved to Rockingham, North Carolina to work for Hannah Pickett Manufacturing Company where he met and married Virginia in 1932. When the plant closed in 1933, they moved to Charlotte to find work in the Highland Park textile mill where Virginia's mother was already employed.

> Plants were in full swing in Charlotte and Horace got a job right away in the weaving department at Highland Park Number Three. About a year later, I went to work as "draw-in-hand," a highly skilled job setting up the pattern for the loom. If you were lucky enough to find a job, you didn't ask questions—you just went to work.
>
> We lived on 36th Street in a big house with my two sisters, Louise and Stella, and my brother, Arthur. My mama rented the house from her first cousin who owned a furniture store. We had four bedrooms, a kitchen, and a dining room with inside plumbing and a kerosene stove for cooking. We heated with coal, which we got from Herron's coal yard. My mother traded (purchased) groceries at the A&P store on Tryon Street.
>
> My mother was a very spiritual person and we would kneel together when we had prayer. My sister, Louise, used to pray, "Dear God, we thank you for what we have, but could you squeeze out a little bit more?" Her prayer was answered when Roosevelt was elected. In Rockingham, I worked for about $1.15 a day, but Roosevelt put us on a 40-hour work-week for 50¢ an hour minimum wage with time-and-a-half for overtime. He made mistakes, but he put a smile on our face.
>
> You know, we were happy. Our diet was good and we didn't go hungry. We were taught responsibility, to be respectful and to not live above our means. My husband and I did not go into debt for anything we did not have enough money to cover. We learned to sew in school, so we made our own clothes. I sewed for all of my family. I designed the patterns from catalogues. Horace had two store-bought white shirts for church and for funerals, but I made all his other shirts and his boxer shorts.
>
> We created our own entertainment. Back then we played the card game Set Back and we played Bingo. We had a small radio and listened to *The Lone Ranger* and *Amos 'n Andy*. When we went to a console, we thought we were "classy." I remember when Charles Crutchfield, a WBT radio announcer, organized the

Briarhoppers in 1935. They were famous for their hillbilly picking.

Saturdays, we went to the swimming pool at the 36th Street YMCA. It was a meeting place for the entire community. Sometimes, we would go uptown for lunch and a movie. The cheapest place to eat was the Canary Cottage. They charged fifteen cents for a hamburger and a nickel for a Coke. My favorite place to eat was Kress's, where you could get lunch and a drink for a quarter.

We were under Blue Law and nothing opened on Sundays, so Horace and I enjoyed riding the trolley to the end of the line and back. At a dime there and a dime back, it was just forty cents for us both. The track came down to North Tryon Street and made a right turn on Eleventh and then turned uphill on Brevard. The corner of Eleventh and Brevard was named "Greasy Corner" because kids would put lard on the train tracks and the trolley would spin on the track and could not make it up the hill.

It was good years. It made us stronger people. I can tell you right now that some of the young people who grew up in the mill village during the Depression are millionaires today. There was a lot of respect for each other among textile people. We would share if there was someone who needed it. I think we felt responsible for each other and watched out after each other's children.

Virginia and Horace worked in textiles until the plant closed in 1966. They later worked for Kendall Manufacturing Company on Carmel Road and lived on Ritch Avenue in North Charlotte. The couple bought a farm in Mint Hill and moved there when they retired.

Her advice: "Do a lot of praying. God gives you the strength to survive."

Making Do

4

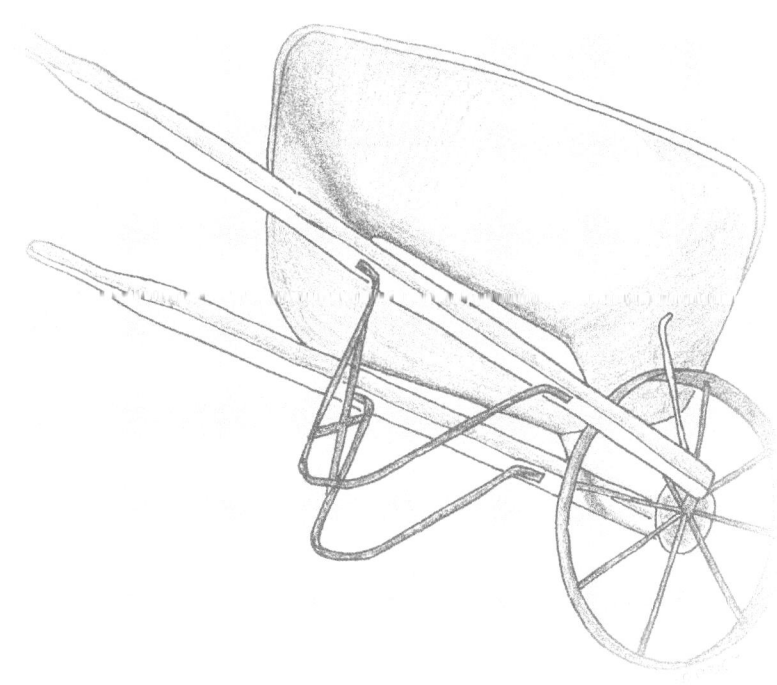

FRED ORR BROWN

Born July 26, 1911

You just had to do on what you had. We had to eat what we grew and try to sell enough to buy what we couldn't raise.

Fred Orr Brown was born on his grandfather's farm on Stumptown Road, northwest of Huntersville. His father, William Brown, married Minnie Cristenberry, the daughter of the veterinarian who took care of cattle all over Mecklenburg County. The couple had four boys and two girls and raised everything they ate on their farm. In the fall, Fred's father also ran a cotton gin in Huntersville.

> You lived on what you had, and if you had the chance to make a few dollars, you did it. We had a corn mill for grinding our corn and we would take a peck from every bushel from others, as a "toll" to pay for grinding it because they did not have any money. When we took our wheat up to Mooresville, they took out a toll to grind it.
>
> You just had to do on what you had. We had to eat what we grew and try to sell enough to buy what we couldn't raise. Cotton was the only thing you get any money out of and it went down to five cents a pound. The boll weevil just about run the cotton business out of this area, so we raised hogs and cows and sold milk, butter, eggs, and vegetables in the stores in Huntersville to buy salt and pepper and Daddy's tobacco.
>
> Most houses had an extra room called the "company room." Salesmen came along on a horse and buggy and would stop and spend the night there and get breakfast the next morning for one dollar.
>
> The first time we went to the circus, Daddy took chickens down to town to sell on North Graham Street to get money enough to take the whole family. The stores in Charlotte had coops in the front for people to buy live chickens and take them home to dress them.
>
> My father had a car, a Chevrolet two door. He owed eighty-five dollars on it and we could not get up the money, so we lost it. When I graduated in 1929, an uncle died and I got his run-down 1924 Model T Ford. I made a Hoover buggy with the old wheels and used it for courting. I also used it for hauling vegetables downtown to pick up a little spending money, but only made four or five dollars profit on a trip.
>
> I also worked at a sawmill, walking three miles each way for one dollar a day. My first job away from home was driving a milk truck for a dairy, seven days a week from four until seven in the morning for forty dollars a month. I gave my mother five dollars a month. The dairy paid their farm help (colored tenants) seventy-five cents a day.
>
> People can't imagine what it was like back in those days. I remember delivering to the S&W Cafeteria. It was the most pathetic thing to see people hunting through the garbage cans out back for something to eat. Anybody that

had a job and did not have to beg or steal was well off.

There wasn't any electricity in our community. We heated our house with fireplaces and there was no inside plumbing, but we didn't know we was in poverty. People respected each other and helped each other and lived closer together. When the reaper came to cut the grain, neighbors helped each other. In the fall, the corn shredder would come through and we did the same thing. Farmers would pile their corn up and we had corn shuckings and the ladies would have a big supper with chicken and dumplings.

The preacher from the Huntersville Associate Reform Presbyterian Church would come out to our house at least once a week with his family and we would give them vegetables and country ham that we cured in a smoke house. That was called "pounding the preacher." He used to say we had the best ham of anybody in the congregation.

I married Martha Elizabeth Duncan in 1938, and we moved to a little house in the pines. I bought a wheelbarrow to clean the yard for $4.10, no tax at the Sears & Roebuck downtown on North College. (They would sell anything they could to make ten cents.) On Sunday afternoons, we would wrap our first boy up in a blanket and take him for a ride in the pasture.

Fred and Martha had three children: Fred Orr, Jr., Jean Elizabeth, and Timothy Duncan. He worked in the fuel oil, heating, and air conditioning business. In 1945, he started the Fred Brown Sunday School class that grew from 8 to 130 members. He still teaches there from time to time today.

His advice: "If you have more of something than you need, share it with someone that needs it."

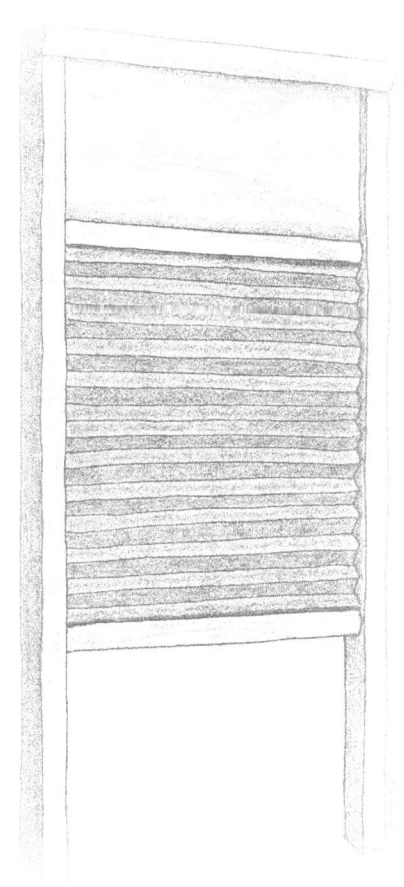

WILLIE STEWART COLEMAN

Born May 27, 1924

We survived because we didn't have no other choice.

Willie Stewart Coleman grew up up in the Crestdale area, before it became a part of Matthews. Back then, it was called Tank Town because that was where the railroad water tank was located. The first inhabitants of the town were former slaves and, although most of the town's residents worked for the railroad, many were sharecroppers too.

Willie's family was more fortunate than most African Americans at the time. Her mother, Ablow, was the mulatto daughter of Bill Weddington, who owned land in the area. Ablow was only thirteen years old when she married Willie's father, Green Lee Stewart, who was eighteen. The couple raised ten children in the Weddington family wood-frame house.

During the Depression, Willie's father was not able to get a job until he did road construction for the WPA. Although her older brother was able-bodied, he could not get a job with the WPA because they would only hire one family member. To survive those times, Willie's grandmother, Maddie, sold off the land, bit by bit.

> If we would have had a farm, we would have had food to eat, but we didn't. Neighbors had pigs and cows and everybody would share what they had. A farmer named Bill Reed gave all of the neighbors molasses that he made. The Coleman family grew wheat and shared their flour and grits with us. We bought buttermilk and butter from Miss Huston, who had a cow. The milk was very thin so she must have watered it down to make enough money to live. We would go and pick red ripper peas for another farmer and received part of the crop which we shared with others. Certain times of the year we picked blackberries down by our well and in the field, too.
>
> We would eat blackberries, biscuits, and fatback meat for breakfast. My mother had a skillet with a top and she would put it in the fireplace with hot coals under and on top of it to bake bread. That was the best tasting bread I ever ate.
>
> When we got a wood stove, we would cut down and carry wood in from the woods in the back of the house. We got sassafras to make tea from those woods, too. There were a lot of things to pick, like wild locust pods and persimmons and creasy greens. We would walk for miles and miles and pick those creasy greens.
>
> Later on, we got a cow that we kept in the shed. My brother milked the cow and I churned the butter. I helped with the wash, too. We would heat the water in the wash pot and put it in the tub with the washboard to wash the clothes with Octagon soap. We made lye soap, too. You boiled the white clothes and sheets and rinsed them three or four times and used bluing in the last tub.
>
> We didn't have an icebox, so we left the food out. No one got sick when we ate it. We put our milk and butter in the spring in the back of the house by the creek. You had to push the tadpoles away with the dipper before you drank the

water from the spring. We used the food grinder to make sausage patties from pig meat and fat, and my mother canned the sausage in jars or put them in corn shucks and hung them in a cold room. We cleaned out the pig guts to make chitlins and we also made liver mush.

My grandparents gave part of their land to build the Matthews Colored Elementary School, so the children could have a school nearby. The schools in Matthews did not go but to the seventh grade, so my older brother had to walk all the way to the Second Ward in Charlotte to finish high school. He couldn't finish because it was just too far to walk.

We survived because we didn't have no other choice. I don't think people today could survive the way we did.

Willie married James Rance Coleman and moved to Charlotte. After raising her own daughter, Daisy, she adopted four other girls, making sure they each finished high school. Active with the Young at Heart group at the Wilmore Community Center, she still gardens in their community garden.

Her advice: "Be thankful for what you have because you couldn't survive like we did."

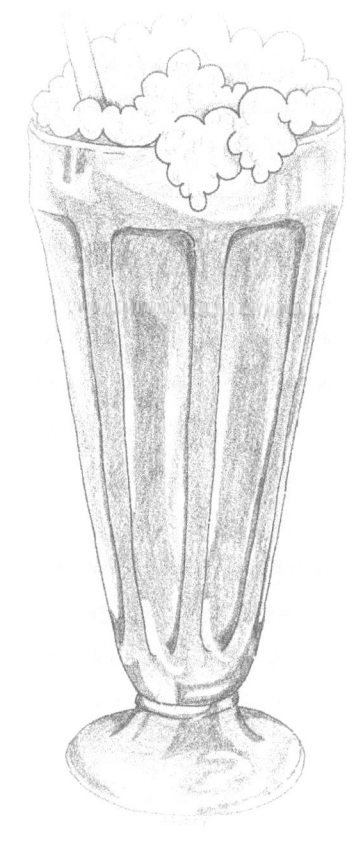

AUBREY FEDERAL

Born September 15, 1920

We had nothing, but we made our own fun.

On November 26, 1929, Aubrey Federal's father, a tile and marble contractor, died of a stroke at the age of fifty. Only nine years old at the time, Aubrey was next to the youngest of four brothers and four sisters. They lived at 1940 Vail Avenue, which is where the front entrance of Mercy Hospital is today. One of the few Catholic families living in Charlotte at the time, Aubrey's older brother, Lennox, was in Europe studying for the priesthood, and his older sister, Margaret, was studying at a Maryland convent.

Since Aubrey's father was heavily insured, their money did not run out until 1933. To help make ends meet, his mother took in boarders. Times were tough for everyone and, on occasion, a family would leave without paying rent. Aubrey and his other siblings found odd jobs to help out at home.

> We all worked, and every dime we made, we gave half of it to Mama. My first job was loading a wheelbarrow with concrete mix from the hopper when they were building the Nurses' Home. Then I worked as a newspaper delivery boy for a penny for every paper I delivered. My first route was from Fourth Street to Morehead, then to Amherst and on to Littleton. The customers paid twenty cents per week and I made seven dollars on a good week.
>
> We had nothing, but we made our own fun. The kids in the neighborhood turned the vacant lot between my house and where they were building the Nurses' Home into a little city. One kid had a lumberyard with scrap lumber from the construction site, and another had a grocery store with berries that he picked. We used bottle caps for money. After dark, we played Kick the Can, which is a form of Hide and Seek. During recess at school, we played Foot and a Half, which is like Leap Frog.
>
> When I turned fifteen, I got a job at the Park Road Pharmacy "hopping the curb" from 3:30 P.M. to midnight for a dollar plus tips a day. Then I got promoted to soda jerk for twelve dollars a week. I always arranged for my study hall to be first period so I could get my homework done.
>
> After that, I went to work at Efird's Department Store as a stock boy and "gofer." I was friends with Mr. Paul Efird, Sr.'s two sons, so I rode to work with him everyday. He offered to pay for my college education, but I declined because I did not want a career in the mercantile business and, if I accepted, I would have felt obligated to do so.
>
> At that time, southerners loved the blacks as individuals but did not care for them as a race. One black man named John Lee had worked for my father and he was like family to us. After my father died, we closed down the family business and my mother brought him into the house and taught him how to cook and clean. John had a wife and thirteen children that we treated like family. When one of his

daughters got married, we all attended the ceremony and Mother furnished all the food for the reception at their house.

Everybody looked out for everybody else during the Depression. It was a good way to grow up. You learned values. Today, every kid wants their own car. All I ever wanted was a pair of skates.

Aubrey married Eva Johnson in 1944 and they had six children: Peg, Miriam, Bill, Chuck, Hank, and Brian. He retired from the contract glass and hardware business after thirty-five years when he sold Federal Glass and Hardware. With his booming voice and Cheshire Cat grin, his witty remarks are usually the center of every conversation, especially when he attends his Class of 1938 Central High School reunion. He stays busy with his hobby, making stained glass ornaments, and staying in touch with his grandchildren via e-mail.

His advice: "You don't have to have a lot to be happy."

CARA HOLBROOK

Born September 1, 1911

You didn't throw things away and you made use of what was around.

Born in the middle of seven siblings on a farm in Stumptown, Cara Holbrook came from a family of farmers. Her father grew up on a farm in downtown Huntersville and her mother near where Huntersville Oaks is today. In 1918, Cara's family moved to the center of Huntersville near the railroad tracks. In addition to farming, her father worked as a rural mail carrier. Cara graduated high school the year the Great Depression hit.

    We did not have a whole lot. Kids today have money in their pockets that we never did. I didn't know a nickel from a quarter. We didn't talk money at home. We knew my parents were doing without as much as we were.

    We always had a garden and chickens, cows, and swine. We had food from what we grew in the garden, which we canned. The kitchen cookstove burned wood and we had wood from our land. Mama was always making clothing for somebody. She made my high school graduation dress.

    You didn't throw things away and you made use of what was around. We took care of the food that we grew and we did not waste food from the kitchen. If there were any leftovers, we used it the next meal. Mama taught us to cook and to sew. The children cleaned house. We had a broom and we swept the wood floors. I did not then, and I do not now, like housekeeping.

    We had several milk cows that I helped milk in the evening. Using a machine called a separator to get the cream off of the milk, we fed the pigs what was left after that. Now they sell it at Food Lion and call it "skim milk." We called it "blue-john" because, when it had no cream, it looked blue. We had a swing churn for making butter, and when it came my turn to churn, which was real often, I usually had a book in my hand. It was a good time to study catechism.

    Papa said, when we were born, my mother started saving money so we could go to college. Six of us graduated from Catawba College and one brother went to the Army because of World War II. As I remember it, I think it was very unusual back then for a family to send that many kids to college.

    With two sisters in college already, I stayed out a year to let my father catch up. I took a business course and found out that was not what I wanted to do. There were not many jobs for girls. There were four of us girls in Catawba College at one time. Two got a degree in home economics and two got elementary school certificates.

    I graduated in 1934 and started teaching in Mecklenburg County out in the country. Another teacher and I lived with the principal and his wife who rented a house close to Oakdale School, part of the Paw Creek school system on the northwest side of Charlotte. I think I paid $22.50 a month room and board. My first yearly salary was $560 for eight months or $70 a month. This was before the

Charlotte city and county schools were consolidated.

    I taught second and third grade combination. Each year, we had to sign a new contract and apply for the job. Every school in the county had its own committee to hire the teachers. I remember walking across the field to talk to the school representative to ask for a job.

    In 1938, I bought my first car, a four-door steel gray Chevrolet, for about $350 from Dwight Cross at Cross Chevrolet in Huntersville. I paid it off at twenty-five dollars a month, but I did not have to make payments during the summer when I wasn't teaching.

Cara taught school for forty-two years and says she can almost guarantee nobody would do that today. Her father was a rural mail carrier for fifty-four years. Her advice for surviving hard times is that you have to work. She says, "If you don't get the job you want first, work that job the best you can and move into what you like, but don't quit working."

Her advice: "Make the most of your opportunities and study while you have a chance."

ELIZABETH GOODMAN KLEIN

Born April 24, 1925

People survived because they were resourceful and thought of all kinds of ways to make money. They were not afraid of work.

Elizabeth Goodman Klein's father, Arthur Goodman, had a friend in the Navy who talked continually about his home in North Carolina. So, after serving in World War I, Goodman moved from Portsmouth, Virginia, to Charlotte to accept a position with the Bon Marche department store. On a business trip to New York, Arthur met Katherine Cohen from Buffalo, New York. They married in 1924 and had two children, Elizabeth and Arthur, Jr.

The couple was among the few Jewish people in Charlotte. They were invited to join the Charlotte Country Club, an institution co-founded half a century earlier by Samuel Wittkowsky, one of the city's leading merchants. Perceiving opportunity in opening a small chain of dime stores serving textile factory employees, Elizabeth's father opened stores in North Wilkesboro and Mooresville with his brother-in-law, Ben Jaffa. Both families moved to Mooresville.

When the Depression caused mills to close, the dime stores went with them. Times were tough and Elizabeth remembers her mother saying, "We were so poor, when you looked up in our house, you saw the sky, and when you looked down, you saw the earth." With no future in retail, her father pursued a career in law. After attending law school at Trinity College, now Duke University, he moved back to Charlotte in 1932 to begin practice. At the time, he was Charlotte's only Jewish attorney.

> My father shared an office in the Law Building with Charlie Bundy. A compassionate lawyer, my father charged little and refused to accept divorce cases, preferring to bring the couples back together. One client referred to him as "Lawyer Jesus."
>
> Charlotte was a small town where some of us were better off than others. We didn't have a lot, but we didn't think of ourselves as rich or poor. We were never hungry, never cold. In our home we learned not to waste and to finish everything on our plates. There was little fancy food on the table, lots of meat loaf, but we didn't feel deprived. It seemed normal at the time. I remember one time when Daddy brought strawberries home as a treat for Mom. He told us, "Your mother loves these so let her have them all."
>
> My grandfather was a physician, so the family had all their medical needs attended to when we summered in Buffalo. He also paid for my dancing lessons. I thought he was the richest man in the world because he had a gardener and a manicurist. In fact, they were patients who couldn't afford to pay my grandfather, so they bartered their services. A tailor who owed money to my grandfather made me a new coat.
>
> When we went to the movies, we saw newsreels of people in line waiting for food and jobs. They looked so poor it just broke your heart. That made us aware of the Depression as did strangers coming to our house to ask for food.

My mother would feed people on the back steps.

Our family maid, Mary Perry, lived in Cherry Town, a black section bordering Myers Park on Queens Road. I think we paid her three dollars a week. She was so ambitious, she took in boarders, ran a café and did everything she could to make ends meet. People survived because they were resourceful and thought of all kinds of ways to make money. They were not afraid of work. They might take photos of you on a pony or sharpen knives or do yard work.

Although our family could no longer afford country club membership, I was invited to parties at the Charlotte and Myers Park Country Clubs. Through all those troubled years, my family participated in many civic and religious activities. My father served as the president of the only Charlotte synagogue, Hebrew United Brotherhood.

In 1942, Elizabeth's father, who went on to serve in the North Carolina House of Representatives, conceived of and founded the Reform congregation, Temple Beth El, which has become the largest Jewish congregation in the Carolinas today. Elizabeth married Walter Klein in 1945 and had four children: Richard, Robert, Kathy, and Betsy. Following in her father's footsteps, Elizabeth served as president of Temple Beth El sisterhood as well as the Hadassah. She was also on the board of the YWCA, the Charlotte Exchange Students Organization, and the Hornets' Nest Council of Girl Scouts of America.

When Hurricane Hugo struck the Charlotte area, Elizabeth thought again of the Great Depression. She said, "People were so good to one another because everyone was in the same boat. When bad things happen, we think of others who are hurting"

Her advice: "Only buy what you can pay for and respect your elders."

MARY WORTH MCKAIN

Born November 18, 1929

We did not have much as kids and we just made do.

Mary Worth Bonum McKain was born less than a month after the Crash of 1929. At the time, her family lived in a duplex in West Charlotte across from Thomasboro School in the Hoskins neighborhood. Her father earned fifteen dollars a week working for A&P Bakery on Cedar Street. Her mother managed to feed a family of four on five dollars of groceries a week. Others were not so fortunate.

>The Sing family that lived across the street from us in the Hoskins neighborhood was an older couple with two sons. They had no work, so we moved to an old country farmhouse off of Rozzelles Ferry Road, where each family could live on one side of a big hall that ran down the center of the house. Everyone was so poor, everybody's nothing was the same as the next person's nothing.
>
>When the Sing family moved out to live with their family, we moved to a two-bedroom duplex on State Street. My father stayed with the bakery and was eventually promoted to supervisor. We moved to a four-family apartment on Avondale (Park Road today). I remember that it had a Murphy bed.
>
>In 1935, we moved back to a house on State Street. The dining room had a circulator heater that used coal. It was my job to fill the bucket from the coal bin that was in the backyard. The kitchen had an icebox, a kerosene stove, and an iron coal-burning laundry heater that heated the water for bathing and washing.
>
>Mother made a lot of pots of vegetable soup that she simmered on the kerosene stove or on the laundry heater when it was warm. Dad always drank the "pot liquor" which was the broth from cooking vegetables. Bread was ten cents a loaf, so we often ate mayonnaise sandwiches.
>
>We did not have much as kids and we just made do. We made paper dolls out of the Sears catalog advertisements and made doll houses out of cardboard boxes, sliding our dolls around in cars made out of books. I remember when I was ten years old and I wanted a Magic Skin baby doll with latex skin. I got the doll and a carriage that Christmas and I was thrilled.
>
>You only got one pair of shoes and you did not stop wearing them until your toes touched the end. We lined the inside with cardboard and repaired them with half soles. I wore the same dress day after day, taking it off when I got home from school. Mother scrubbed our clothes in a tub on a washboard. My sister, Patsy, was fifteen months older than me and we shared everything, even a bicycle. We slept together in the same bed until she got married.
>
>I remember visiting my grandmother for a few weeks every summer. She lived on a farm in Magnolia in eastern North Carolina. She did not trust the banks and buried her money in a jar in the yard.
>
>In 1939, we bought a lot on Dogwood Avenue and Mother went to work at

Belk's Basement. We had Mr. Moretz build us a house for $3,100.

Mary Worth says she is very thankful that she grew up in a time when she did not have anything. When hard times visited her again in the '70s, she says she made it because she knew how to be frugal. On her own, with two children still at home to support, she rented rooms and was on food stamps. She said, "I was thankful for what I had."

Her advice: "Save money rather than spending it so freely."

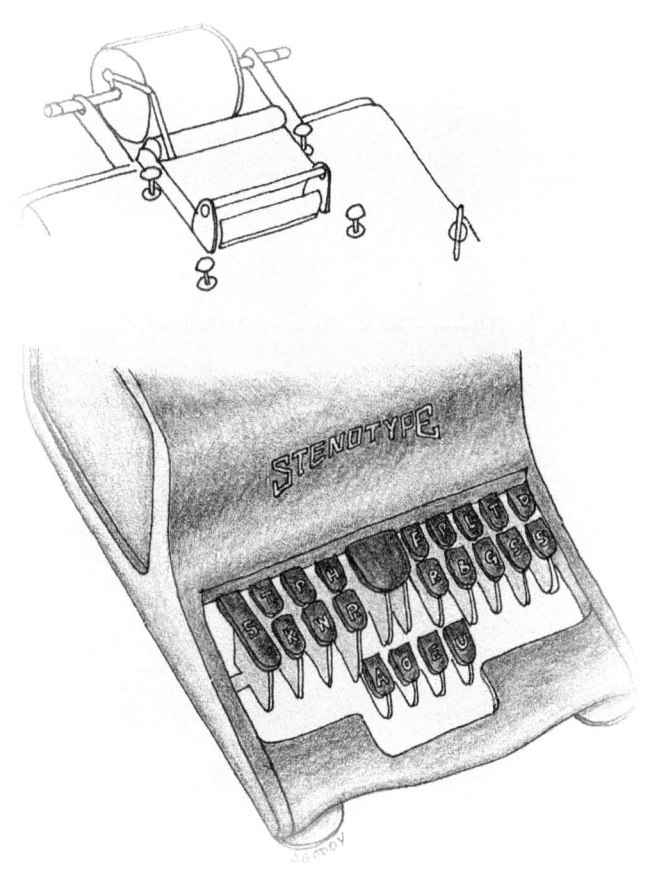

MELBA RIDENHOUR MOORE

Born May 10, 1912

What we didn't have, we didn't miss.

Melba Ridenhour Moore and her sister, Ruth, who was thirteen months older, grew up in a three-bedroom house on Tenth Avenue in the Fourth Ward. Her mother, Maggie, came from the Concord/Kannapolis area and her father, Earl Ridenhour, was from around Albemarle, North Carolina. He worked at G.G. Ray Heating Company and, although he did not have as much work during the Depression, he went to work everyday and brought home a paycheck every week. They were more fortunate than others and her mother never turned anyone away who came to the door for food.

>We had a lot of beggars, mostly men. Mother would scramble them an egg and give them a piece of buttered toast. She always made cookies, cakes and pies to give to the postman and the garbage man and friends. I remember her oatmeal cookies most of all.
>
>What we didn't have, we didn't miss. Children these days get a whole lot of toys, but we got useful things at Christmas time. We would get galoshes and a raincoat and be thrilled. Mother's sister, Aunt Lilly, lived on a farm in Kannapolis. She would bring us eggs and food from the farm. My mother was very close to her sister, so she would take my sister and me to spend the summers up on the farm. We stayed in a tent that we pitched in their yard, right next to the house. Mother and Aunt Lilly would can food and do everything together.
>
>We made our own fun. In the evening, the family sat around a big radio called a Majestic and listened to funny family shows like *Amos 'n Andy*. There were twelve teenagers in our neighborhood and we formed the "Dizzy Dozen" club. We had meetings and parties and put on formals and dances with cookies and punch.
>
>In 1930, I went to Women's College of the University of North Carolina in Greensboro to take a business course. Stenotype had just come out and I bought the first one made for $100. I worried about asking my parents for the money, but they gave it to me.
>
>My father's company had a basketball team that played at the YMCA. One day, when I was visiting from college, he told my sister and me that one of the employee's nephews, Paul Moore from Wesley Chapel, North Carolina, was playing on the team. We went and cheered from the balcony. After the game, they came up to meet us. I started dating Paul and we became engaged. He moved to Charlotte and starting working at Belk's in the furniture department.
>
>We married in 1932 and lived in my parents' house. They made a four-room apartment on one side of the house and we paid them rent. Then, Paul started to work for the same heating company as my father. He had a beautiful disposition and a lot of customers liked him. After a while, he bought a building

on East Eighth Street and started his own business called Moore Sheet Metal and Heating. He worked on the S&W Cafeteria uptown and did a lot of sheet metal work for restaurant kitchens.

My husband always had work because people liked him. We lived on what we made and I helped by budgeting our money. None of our friends tried to outdo each other. We built our own home on Avondale Avenue on the corner where Park Road started. In 1933, we had our first child, Carole.

The Moores remained in Charlotte and had a second daughter, Sandra, in 1942. They were very involved in the Tenth Avenue Presbyterian Church, where Melba went as a child. Melba later became one of the founding members of the Avondale Presbyterian Church, where she continued to actively volunteer. Staying in touch with her friends from the "Dizzy Dozen" for many years, she says her daughter, Sandra, is now friends with one of their daughters.

Her advice: "Be pleasant to everyone, young or old."

R. (ROBERT) POWELL MAJORS

Born December 12, 1906

We survived because we lived within our means.

Born in Poole, Kentucky, R. Powell Majors' family eventually moved to St. Petersburg, Florida in 1921. Graduating with a degree in Business Administration from the University of Florida in 1928, he accepted a job for $125 a month with Peat Marwick and Mitchell, a public accounting and auditing firm in Charlotte. He had to sell his tuxedo for eighteen dollars in order to have enough money to move there. For the first two months, he stayed at the YMCA on the corner of Second and South Tryon Streets and then rented a room with a college friend in a private home on Greenway Avenue off of Caswell Road, close to Mercy Hospital. He rode the streetcar to work, buying four tickets for a quarter.

>The accounting business was fairly good until February 1931 when I became unemployed. I knew it was going to hit me because income tax was due by March 15 and, by February 1, we did not have anything to do. Everybody was broke. The government did not take taxes out of paychecks at that time, and if you did not make $1,500 dollars a year, you were exempt from federal income tax.
>
>After one week, I got a job for the Veterans Administration who needed extra help paying off a bonus to WWI veterans. I worked from three o'clock in the afternoon to eleven o'clock at night. When Tryon Drug Store went bankrupt, the receiver hired me to keep the books from 8:00 in the morning to 2:30 in the afternoon. Mr. Holmes, one of the former Tryon Drug partners, opened Park Place Pharmacy and hired me to work on Saturday and Sunday, teaching his daughter to keep the books.
>
>By that time, I was living with the Hal Bobbitt family and was working so much that dating was out of the question. I did not even have time to get a haircut. All of those jobs were temporary, so I took advantage of every opportunity that came my way.
>
>At the end of May 1931, my jobs ran out, so I went to Florida to visit my family in St. Petersburg for two weeks' vacation. I did not tell them I was unemployed because they had problems of their own. Their real estate business went kaput way before the Depression.
>
>When I returned to Charlotte, the Bobbitts woke me early the next morning because Mr. Bobbitt's brother, Bill, wanted to talk to me about a job. He was an attorney for Independent Trust Company and they had foreclosed on a loan to a finance company in Hendersonville, They had to liquidate the collateral and the CEO of the finance company had an unsavory reputation, so they wanted an honest person to handle the pocketbook. The vice president interviewed me on the drive to Asheville and I got hired.
>
>A lot of people were out of work, so my job was not very pleasant. I was trying to get money out of people who did not have it, so I had to sue them. I

stayed there one year to the hour and moved back to Charlotte to work for Peat Marwick. After I did an audit at Southern Asbestos Company, they offered me forty dollars a week to work for them.

I married Dorothy Alma Fortune in 1933. The first year we were married, I worked out a daily form to put down what we spent every day to develop a budget. Dot took five dollars a week and bought all of the groceries. She had milk delivered to the door and the laundry, too. Our rent was thirty-five dollars a month and I was making thirty-six dollars a week. I smoked in those days and bought cigarettes for $1.25 a carton. In 1934, we had to buy a refrigerator for nine dollars a month. It was the first time I was in debt and it drove me crazy.

We survived because we lived within our means. One of our favorite eating places was Holmes Restaurant on South Tryon Street, just below the Catholic church. They had good food and it was real reasonable. For thirty-five cents, you could go to Thacker's on South Tryon for a meat and two vegetables. You could get the same at the S&W Cafeteria in 1935.

I was affected by the Depression. I still turn out lights and conserve on everything. We raised our two children, Robert, Jr. and Nancy, that way.

After resigning from Southern Asbestos in 1943, Powell went on to work for Lance, Inc. for twenty-five years. A civic-minded institution, Lance encouraged him to get involved in the community. As a member of the Charlotte Rotary Club for sixty-eight years, he served as their president in 1946 and as president of the American Red Cross in 1953. After he retired, he worked part time for Central Piedmont Community College as a fundraiser for nineteen years.

His advice: "Get an education and learn to take care of what money you have. Be moderate in everything."

Facts, Figures & Photos

Charlotte / Mecklenburg During the Great Depression

POPULATION

1920	Charlotte 46,338	Mecklenburg 80,695
1930	Charlotte 82,675	Mecklenburg 127,971
1940	Charlotte 100,899	Mecklenburg 151,826

TIMELINE

1929

- October 29 – "Black Tuesday" *New York Times* index of industrial stocks drops nearly 40 points, the worst drop in Wall Street history to that point.
- May 6 – Charlotte's official flag is designated (blue field with seal in white.)
- Charlotte's Greek community establishes an Orthodox church on South Boulevard.
- A bitter struggle ensues at the Loray textile mill as union organizers come to Gastonia. Police Chief Aderholt is shot and killed and the trial is moved to Mecklenburg County.

1930

- More than 3.2 million people are unemployed nationwide.
- October – Committee for Unemployment Relief is formed.
- Average cost of groceries: bread—8¢ a loaf; butter—25¢ a pound; flour—3¢ a pound; milk—14¢ a quart.
- Pilot Gene Brown flies first air mail delivery into Charlotte.
- Charlotte becomes the largest city in the state with a population of 82,675.
- First National Bank, Mechanics & Farmers Bank, and Independence National Bank close.

1931

- January 7 – Committee for Unemployment Relief reports 4–5 million out of work.
- December 11 – New York Bank of the United States collapses.

1932

- Number of unemployed U.S. workers reaches 13 million.
- Hit songs: *Shanty in Old Shanty Town* and *Brother Can You Spare a Dime?*
- Charlotte Symphony Orchestra is organized.

- July 28 – "Bonus Army Riot" with 20,000 World War I veterans in Washington, DC.
- Congress establishes the Reconstruction Finance Corporation, which lends $2 billion to banks, insurance companies, building and loan associations, agricultural credit organizations and railroads. Critics call it the "millionaires' dole."
- November – Franklin Delano Roosevelt elected U. S. President in a landslide victory.

1933

- January 23 – The 20th Amendment is ratified.
- January 31 – Adolf Hitler is named Chancellor of Germany.
- March 31 – Reforestation Relief Act creates the Civilian Conservation Corps (CCC).
- November 8 – Civil Works Administration (CWA) is created by executive order.
- December 5 – The 21st Amendment is ratified and Prohibition is repealed.
- Charlotte's Lakewood Park is closed.

1934

- Charlotte has first interracial baseball game as the white Highland Park Mill team meets the North Charlotte Black Yankees. The *Charlotte Observer* reports that Highland Park wins, 11-10. The *Charlotte News* reports that the Black Yankees win, 10-7!
- Southern Tenant Farmers Union is founded.
- Charlotte Mayor Douglas obtains federal funding to rebuild U.S. Mint as a museum.

1935

- April 8 – Emergency Appropriations Relief Act passes, creating the Works Progress Administration (WPA).
- July 5 – National Labor Relations Act is passed.
- WPA begins building Memorial Stadium on the former Charlotte City Waterworks site.
- Work begins on the Blue Ridge Parkway.
- November 5 – Parker Brothers Company releases new board game, "Monopoly."
- President Franklin D. Roosevelt signs the Social Security Act.
- Musicals like *Top Hat* with Ginger Rogers and Fred Astaire fill movie theaters.

1936

- Charlotte American Legion Memorial Stadium opens.
- President Franklin D. Roosevelt is guest of honor at Charlotte's "Green Pastures" rally
- October 22 – The Mint Museum opens.
- Charlotte's first public airport, Douglas Municipal Airport, is built and named in honor of Mayor Ben Douglas.
- "Father of Bluegrass Music," Bill Monroe, makes first recording in Charlotte warehouse.
- President Roosevelt is elected to second term, winning every state but Maine and Vermont.
- November 23 – *LIFE Magazine* begins publication.

1937

- The first Shrine Bowl game pits the best high school players from North and South Carolina against each other in what will become an annual football rivalry. Charlotte games produce largest annual contribution to any Shriners' Children's Hospital in the U.S.
- Benny Goodman is labeled "The King of Swing" with his boogie-woogie big-band sound.

1938

- January – President Roosevelt establishes the March of Dimes.
- November 1– Seabiscuit sets a new track record, beating War Admiral by four lengths in just over one minute fifty-six seconds for the one and three-sixteenths mile.
- Buses replace trolleys and "Old #85" makes its last run in Charlotte.

1939

- April 30 – New York World's Fair opens.
- June 30 – Charlotte Public Library closes when voters failed to approve appropriation and does not reopen until July 1940 when tax levy is passed.
- September 1 – World War II begins in Europe when Germany invades Poland.
- *The Grapes of Wrath* by John Steinbeck is published.
- Popular award-winning movies *Gone With the Wind* and *The Wizard of Oz* are released.
- Charlotte Mayor, Ben E. Douglas, authorizes first public housing to be built in the city.

Central High School 1929

Page from Central High School yearbook, 1939

Huntersville High School date unknown

Central High School Class of 1939 belt buckle

Cotton Warehouse, 1930s

Kress 5 n 10, 1920s

Trolley Uptown 1930s

WPA Independence Park 1940

Lentz Grocery 1930s

Uptown, Charlotte became largest city in North Carolina 1930

Textile Mill sale 1930s

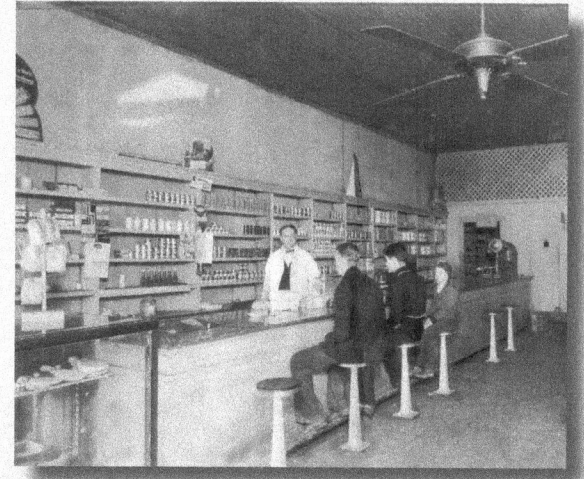
Baldwin's Cafe circa 1929

President Franklin D. Roosevelt speaks at "Green Pastures" Rally in Charlotte, 1936

More Keys to Surviving the Great Depression

&

Advice for Future Generations

More Keys to Surviving the Great Depression

We interviewed many more individuals for this project than appear in this book. Due to space limitations, everyone's stories could not be included in the exhibit, but we wanted to share some of these additional words of wisdom:

"We never did have any store bought things. It wasn't much different before the Depression."

Ruby Black

"It was important to respect authority because we all had to live together and get along."

Dorothy Cochrane

"We ate a lot of biscuits and pinto beans and boiled potatoes."

Earl Cox

"My parents were hard workers. They got out and did what they had to do to keep things together."

Betty Cowan

"I think about mother and father scraping the bottom of the barrel, but they never let on to the children, even though I am sure they wanted to complain."

Elsie Henley

"Families were closer then and we looked out for one another. The people that lived in our neighborhood were like one big family."

Mae Alexander Johnson

"If you knew somebody, you could get a job."

Billie Kanupke

"We did not lose a lot because we did not have a lot."

Virginia Jennings Walker

"If you didn't have to have it, you didn't buy it."

Mason Wallace

Advice for Future Generations

"Do like my family did, work and help other people."

Evelyn Allen

"The simplest thing in the world is to just love and respect people."

Jesse Atkins

"If you have more of something than you need, share it with someone that needs it."

Fred Orr Brown

"Today, too much of our values are placed on material things, which can disappear, but families and friends last forever."

Sarah Bryant

"Be thankful for what you have because you couldn't survive like we did."

Willie Coleman

"If you come from a loving family, you can survive."

Price Davis

"The real values in life are the ones that stick with you—not material things, but family."

Ann Mauldin Elliot

"Advice to this generation: You don't have to have a lot to be happy."

Aubrey Federal

"Don't try to outdo each other. Share what you have."

Katie Grier

"If you cannot afford cash to pay for it, don't purchase it."

Skinny Harris

"Make the most of your opportunities and study while you have a chance."

Cara Holbrook

"The family is the greatest thing of all."

Steve Karres

"Only buy what you can pay for and respect your elders."

Elizabeth Klein

"Be active and belong to your church, whatever denomination. Hold onto your family ties, it means a lot."

Bett Kofinas

"The best way to survive is to get known and to get involved."

Jerry Levine

"You have to be able to see what is coming next and move on to the next thing."

J. Henry McGill

"Save money rather than spending it so freely."

Mary Worth McKain

"Get an education and learn to take care of what money you have. Be moderate in everything."

R. Powell Majors

"Give your very best effort in whatever you do. If you worked for it and earned it, you could hold your head high."

Martha Mitchell

"Be pleasant to everyone, young or old."

Melba Moore

"Do a lot of praying. God gives you the strength to survive."

Virginia Moore

"Learn to respect those who are older and who have more wisdom and experience."

Dewitt Reid

"Save money; don't buy everything you want."

Jean Surratt

"Nowadays, everybody tries to go to school to learn how to make money. What people really need to learn is how to spend money wisely."

Mary Anna Turner

"The best thing to do with the money you make is to save what you can."

R.D. Wilke

Afterword

Going into this project with the ups and downs of our economy in mind, I hoped to discover a few secrets to financial security. During the interviews, I listened for the types of business that succeeded and real estate that retained its value. The wisdom I gleaned from the participants turned out to be something quite different from what I expected. Although I heard good advice about work ethics and sticking to it, the prevailing common thread to survival turned out to be something you could not buy, much less accomplish on your own.

What appeared to hold everyone together through the lean times was more about values than things of value. The ability to survive came from extended families, close-knit communities, and neighborhood churches. I also learned that survival was not about accumulating wealth but, as Katie Grier put it, sharing what you had.

Perhaps, with roots in rural farming, the greater Charlotte area already had established the sense of camaraderie and community, so sharing and watching out for each other was second nature. Even those that lived in the city knew the importance of looking out for others. People everywhere respected each other, particularly their elders.

Of course, being practical and learning to do without helped a great deal during that era, too. (Who does not have stories about their parents walking for miles and saving pieces of soap and tin foil?) Although some of the participants advised to avoid spending what you did not have and to save what you can, most of the advice for future generations centered on the importance of family, church and community ties. As they all pointed out, the neighborhoods were small and everyone knew each other. Everyone looked out for one another's children, so there was truly no child left behind.

In our modern society, it appears that this strong sense of community, where everybody knows each other, is being mowed over with rapid growth and bigger-is-better attitudes. I do not know about you but, after listening to these stories from my elders, I am convinced that the best investment I can make is to bank my time and efforts in my family and my community.

Acknowledgments

I am forever grateful to my parents, Jack and Sandra Babich, for their encouragement and example to be both creative and to care about others. My wonderful husband, David, continues that support, assuring me that I can get anything done if I take it one step at a time.

Thankfully, Pam Meister, President and CEO of The Charlotte Museum of History, advocated for the *Personal Legacies* project, to the point of bringing it to fruition. Working in partnership with the Museum staff, particularly Kris Carmichael, who became my creative "soul mate," was what gave the project wings.

I am indebted to Jen Crickenberger who followed me from pillar to post to capture the images of the many individuals and their artifacts to create her beautiful montages and to Jessi Godoy for her wonderful illustrations. Many thanks as well to many individuals, the Charlotte Observer and The Charlotte Museum of History for permission to use their photographs. Those images bring so much more to the stories than just words alone could express.

I am grateful to Susan Alford and the staff at CPCC Press for welcoming the idea for the book and working to see it through to publication. It was also an honor to receive an Arts & Science Council Regional Artist Project Grant to help fund the production and marketing of this book.

Many members of the community assisted me in finding individuals to interview for the project, including Rita Rouse from the Public Library System of Charlotte/ Mecklenburg County; Linda Miller, ombudsman from Centralina Council of Governments; Marnie Moskowitz from the Jewish Federation of Greater Charlotte, and James Ross with the Wednesday Morning Breakfast Club. Tim Ross, associate producer with WFAE *Charlotte Talks* and Jeri Krentz and Cliff Harrington, editors with *The Charlotte Observer*, were among many members of the media that announced our programs in the library branches. Thanks to the Carriage Club, Huntersville Oaks, Sharon Towers, and Aldersgate for hosting some of the sessions as well.

Most of all, I want to thank all of the participants who volunteered to share their hearts and memories, their lessons, and advice. Although not all of you are included in these pages, I was delighted to get to know you and hope you will continue to tell your stories.

There are no beginnings and endings to the birth of a book, and I imagine, for the sake of brevity, that I may have left out some of the individuals who inspired and helped me along the way. Please know that I appreciate your efforts to make this project and book possible.

The Author

A professional writer and storyteller for over thirty years, Robin A. Edgar conducts reminiscence-writing workshops based on her book, *In My Mother's Kitchen: An Introduction to the Healing Power of Reminiscence*. She teaches in a variety of venues including schools and universities and arts centers such as the prestigious John C. Campbell Folk School and often often serves as a national keynote speaker and workshop facilitator for organizations such as Hospice and the Alzheimer's Association.

As an Arts & Science Council Artist-in-the-Workplace, Robin worked with Carolinas Medical Center to publish their 20th anniversary book, *Celebrating 20 Years and Growing*. The recipient of the 2006 ASC Regional Artist Project Grant, she is the project coordinator for the Personal Legacies: Surviving the Great Depression, Charlotte / Mecklenburg 1929–1939 exhibition at The Charlotte Museum of History.

In a similar project with WaterWorks Visual Arts Center in Salisbury, North Carolina, she collaborated with photographer, Jenn Gardner, and Rowan-Salisbury middle and high school students on the book, *Object Stories*. The compilation of photographs and stories about personal heroes served as a catalog for an exhibition with the same title.

The mother of three grown children, Robin lives in Charlotte, North Carolina with her husband, David.

The Photographer

Jennifer Crickenberger is a professional fine art and freelance photographer based in Charlotte, North Carolina. She obtained her bachelor of fine art in Studio Arts from UNC Charlotte where she created large bodies of photographic work and interactive installation pieces that comment on the concepts of memory and mass media.

Her work has been exhibited in several Charlotte area shows including "Scale," "Emancipated Logic," "Fusion," and "Sanskrit." She is an outreach photography instructor for The Light Factory: Museum of Contemporary Photography, where her classes motivate young people to question sociopolitical issues and express their opinions through conceptual photography.

The Illustrator

Jessi Godoy currently works as a freelance artist and designer. Graduating with a bachelor of arts in Studio Art and a Master of Science in Interior Design from Florida State University, she has also worked professionally in commercial and residential interior design.

She previously collaborated with Robin Edgar as the illustrator for the book, *In My Mother's Kitchen: An Introduction to the Healing Power of Reminiscence.* Jessi lives in southern Arizona with her husband, Erwin.

Charlotte / Mecklenburg
1929–1939

at

The
CHARLOTTE MUSEUM
of HISTORY

3500 Shamrock Drive
Charlotte, NC 28215
www.charlottemuseum.org

If you are interested in having *Personal Legacies*
Project Director Robin Edgar come to your
school, library, or historic organization,
contact the museum at 704-651-7156
or go to www.robinedgar.com.

www.ingramcontent.com/pod-product-compliance
Lightning Source LLC
Chambersburg PA
CBHW061820290426
44110CB00027B/2930